ACT MATHEMATICS

Improving College Admission Test Scores

Contributing Writers

Ralph Fech
L. Ramadeen
Matthew Mitkus
Dr. John Sico, Jr.

Copyright © 2004 Instructivision, Inc. Revised 2006
ISBN 973-156749-571-3
Printed in Canada

Instructivision, Inc., P.O. Box 2004, 16 Chapin Road, Pine Brook, NJ 07058
Telephone 973-575-9992 or 888-551-5144; fax 973-575-9134, website: www.instructivision.com

TABLE OF CONTENTS

INTRODUCTION

The American College Testing Program (ACT) is a comprehensive system of data collection, processing, and reporting designed to assist students in the transition from high school to college. The academic tests—in English, mathematics, reading, and science reasoning—emphasize reasoning and problem-solving skills. The test items represent scholastic tasks required in college level work and are oriented toward the major areas of high school and college instructional programs.

ACT questions are designed to measure a wide range of abilities and knowledge. Consequently, some of the items are difficult while others are fairly easy. A background of strong academic courses combined with a worthwhile review will enable you to meet this challenge successfully.

The Mathematics Test

The Mathematics Test is a 60-question, 60-minute examination that measures mathematics reasoning abilities. The test focuses on the solution of practical quantitative problems that are encountered in high school and some college courses. The test uses a work-sample approach that measures mathematical skills in the context of simple and realistic situations. Each of the multiple choice questions has five alternative responses. To determine the answer to the problem, examine the choices, and select the correct response.

Five content subdivisions are classified in the Mathematics Test (see chart, page v). The 60 test questions reflect an appropriate balance of content and skills (low, middle, and high difficulty) and range of performance. Because there is no penalty for guessing, answer every question. There are no trick questions; however, in some problems, you may have to go through a number of steps in order to find the correct answer.

In order to perform efficiently and accurately throughout the examination, you must understand and apply fundamental mathematical concepts. Spending too much time on any one item is unwise. On the average, spend about one minute on each question. Any remaining time should be spent in completing unanswered questions or reviewing previous work.

How to Use the Mathematics Workbook

This workbook consists of the introduction, a glossary of terms, formulas, three practice tests, and skill builders, and additional questions for review.

Glossary: The glossary defines commonly used mathematical expressions and many special and technical words.

Formulas: Formulas that are commonly applied to mathematical problems are listed in a separate section. This section can be used as a convenient reference for formulas relating to geometric shapes and algebraic functions.

Practice Tests: There are three full-length practice tests. Under actual testing conditions, you are allowed 60 minutes for the entire test. The instructions should be followed carefully.

Skill Builders: The skill builders describe and illustrate each of the content areas in the Mathematics Test. The skill builders are divided into sections, each of which relates to one of the principal categories covered in the test. Each skill builder consists of a series of examples, orientation exercises, practice exercises, and a practice test.

The answers to the sample tests and the skill builder exercises and practice tests are not found in the Student Workbook. They are included in the Teacher Manual.

How the ACT is Scored

The "raw" score of 1 point for each correct answer will be converted to a "scale" score. The scale on which ACT academic test scores are reported is 1-36, with a mean (or average) of 18, based on a nationally representative sample of October-tested 12th grade students who plan to enter two-year or four-year colleges or universities. The scale for each subscore is 1-18, with a mean of 9. A guidance counselor will be glad to answer questions regarding the scoring process and the score reports.

Math Strategies

1. Answer all questions. First do those problems with which you are most familiar and which seem the easiest to solve, and then answer those you find more difficult.

2. Practice pacing yourself. Try to solve most of the problems in less than one minute each.
3. Pay close attention to the information in each problem. Use the information that is important in solving the problem.
4. If you are making an educated guess, try to eliminate any choices that seem unreasonable.
5. If the item asks for an equation, check to see if your equation can be transformed into one of the choices.
6. Always work in similar units of measure.
7. Sketch a diagram for reference when feasible.
8. Sometimes there is more than one way to solve a problem. Use the method that is most comfortable for you.
9. Use your estimation skills to make educated guesses.
10. Check your work.

Items are classified according to five content categories. These categories and the approximate proportion of the test devoted to each are given below.

1. *Pre-Algebra.* Items in this category are based on operations with whole numbers, decimals, fractions, and integers. They also may require the solution of linear equations in one variable.

2. *Elementary Algebra.* Items in this category are based on operations with algebraic expressions. The most advanced topic in this category is the solution of quadratic equations by factoring.

3. *Intermediate Algebra and Coordinate Geometry.* Items in this category are based on graphing in the standard coordinate plane or on other topics from intermediate algebra such as operations with integer exponents, radical expressions and rational expressions, the quadratic formula, and linear inequalities in two variables.

4. *Plane Geometry.* Items in this category are based on the properties and relations of plane figures.

5. *Trigonometry.* Items in this category are based on right triangle trigonometry, graphs of the trigonometric functions, and basic trigonometric identities.

ACT Assessment Mathematics Test
60 items, 60 minutes

Content Area	Proportion of Test	Number of Items
Pre-Algebra and Elementary Algebra	.40	24
Intermediate Algebra and Coordinate Geometry	.30	18
Plane Geometry	.23	14
Trigonometry	.07	4
Total	1.00	60

Scores reported:

Pre-Algebra/Elementary Algebra (24 items)

Intermediate Algebra/Coordinate Geometry (18 items)

Plane Geometry/Trigonometry (18 items)

Total possible maximum raw test score (60 items) is 60. Because the formula for calculating the final score varies slightly each year we have not included this information here.

ABSCISSA

An ordered pair (*x*, *y*) specifying the distance of points from two perpendicular number lines (*x* and *y*-axis). E.g., in (4, 6) the first number—the *x* number (4)—is called the *abscissa*. The second number—the *y* number (6)—is called the *ordinate*.

ABSOLUTE VALUE

The absolute value of a number *x*, written |*x*|, is the number without its sign; e.g., |+8| = 8, |0| = 0, or |-4| = 4. On a number line it can be interpreted as the distance from zero, regardless of direction.

ACUTE ANGLE

An angle whose measure is less than 90 degrees.

ACUTE TRIANGLE

A triangle whose three angles each measure less than 90 degrees.

ADDITIVE INVERSE

The additive inverse of a number *a* is the number -*a* for which *a* + (-*a*) = 0. You can think of the additive inverse of a number as its opposite; e.g., the additive inverse of -5 is +5 because (-5) + (+5) = 0.

ADJACENT ANGLES

Two angles having a common vertex and a common side between them.

ALGORYTHM

A finite set of instructions having the following characteristics:
- Precision. The steps are precisely stated.
- Uniqueness. The intermediate results of each step of execution are uniquely defined and depend only on the inputs and the results of the preceding steps.
- Finiteness. The algorithm stops after finitely many instructions have been executed.
- Input. The algorithm receives input.
- Output. The algorithm produces output.
- Generality. The algorithm applies to a set of inputs.

ALTERNATE INTERIOR ANGLES

Two angles formed by a line (the transversal) that cuts two parallel lines. The angles are interior angles on opposite sides of the transversal and do not have the same vertex.

ALTITUDE of a triangle

A line segment drawn from a vertex point perpendicular to the opposite side (base); the length is referred to as the height of the triangle. In a right triangle, the altitude is one of the legs. In an obtuse triangle, the altitude meets the base at a point on its extension.

ANGLE

A figure formed by two rays that have the same endpoint. The rays are the sides of the angle. The endpoint of each ray is called the vertex.

ARC

A segment or piece of a curve.

AREA

The measure of a surface; e.g., number of square units contained within a region. Area of a rectangle = length times width.

ASSOCIATION

A special grouping of numbers to make computation easier; e.g., $245 \times (5 \times 2) = 245 \times 10 = 2,450$ instead of $(245 \times 5) \times 2 = 1,225 \times 2 = 2,450$.

ASSOCIATIVE LAW

of addition: The way numbers are grouped does not affect the sum; e.g.,

$$a + (b + c) = (a + b) + c$$
$$5 + (6 + 3) = (5 + 6) + 3$$
$$5 + 9 = 11 + 3$$
$$14 = 14$$

of multiplication: The way numbers are grouped does not affect the product; e.g.,

$$a(bc) = (ab)c$$
$$3(4 \times 5) = (3 \times 4)5$$
$$3(20) = (12)5$$
$$60 = 60$$

AVERAGE

The average of a group of numbers is found by adding all the quantities being averaged and then dividing by the number of quantities being averaged; e.g., 60, 70, 80, and 90.

$$\text{Average} = \frac{60 + 70 + 80 + 90}{4} = \frac{300}{4} = 75$$

AXES GRAPHING
Two perpendicular lines used as a reference for ordered pairs.

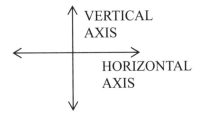

BASE of a power
The number to which an exponent is attached. In the expression x^3, x is the base, 3 is the exponent.

BASE of a triangle
The side of a triangle to which the altitude is drawn.

BASE ANGLES of a triangle
The two angles that have the base of the triangle as a common side.

BINOMIAL
An algebraic expression consisting of two terms: $3x + 5y$ is a binomial.

BISECT
To divide in half.
Bisect an angle: to draw a line through the vertex dividing the angle into two equal angles.
Bisect a line segment: to divide the line into two equal line segments.

CENTER of a circle
The fixed point in a plane about which a curve is equally distant. The center of a circle is the point from which every point on the circumference is equidistant.

CENTRAL ANGLE
In a circle, an angle whose vertex is the center and whose sides are radii.

CHORD
A chord of a circle is a line segment joining any two points on the circle.

CIRCLE
The set of points in a plane at a given distance (the radius) from a fixed point in the plane (called the center).

CIRCUMFERENCE
The distance around a circle.

CIRCUMSCRIBED
To draw a line around a figure; e.g., a circle circumscribed around a triangle is a circle that passes through each vertex of the triangle.

COEFFICIENT
A coefficient is the number before the letters in an algebraic term, in $3xyz$, 3 is the coefficient.

COMBINATION
The arrangement of a number of objects into groups; e.g., A, B, and C into groups AB, AC, and BC.

COMMON DENOMINATOR
A common denominator is a common multiple of the denominators of the fractions. A common denominator for $\frac{1}{2}$ and $\frac{1}{3}$ is 6 because $\frac{1}{2} = \frac{3}{6}$ and $\frac{1}{3} = \frac{2}{6}$.

COMMUTATIVE LAW
of addition: The order of the numbers does not affect the sum; e.g.,
$$a + b = b + a$$
$$8 + 3 = 3 + 8$$
$$11 = 11$$
of multiplication: The order of the numbers does not affect the product; e.g.,
$$ab = ba$$
$$(6)(8) = (8)(6)$$
$$48 = 48$$

COMPLEMENTARY ANGLES
Two angles whose sum is a right angle (90°).

COMPOSITE NUMBER
A composite number is a natural number that can be divided by 1 or by some number other than itself. A composite number has factors other than itself and 1; e.g.,
$$4 = (4)(1) \text{ and } (2)(2)$$
$$6 = (6)(1) \text{ and } (3)(2)$$

CONE
A space figure with one flat face (known as a base) that is a circle and with one other face that is curved.

CONGRUENT

triangles: two triangles that can be made to coincide (symbol ≅).
lines: lines that are the same length.
angles: angles that have the same measure in degrees.

CONSECUTIVE INTEGERS

Numbers that follow in order; e.g., 1, 2, 3, 4, 5, 6, etc. Even consecutive integers = 2, 4, 6, 8, ... Odd consecutive integers = 1, 3, 5, 7, ...

CONSECUTIVE INTERIOR ANGLES

Two angles of a polygon with a common side.

CONSTANT

A symbol representing a single number during a particular discussion; e.g., $x^2 + x + 5$ has +5 as the constant that does not vary in value.

CONVERSION

To change the units of an expression; e.g., *convert* 2 hours and 3 minutes to 123 minutes.

COORDINATES OF A POINT

An ordered pair (x, y) specifying the distance of points from two perpendicular number lines (x and y-axis); e.g., in (4, 6) the first number—the x number (4)—is called the abscissa. The second number—the y number (6)—is called the ordinate.

CORRESPONDING ANGLES

Two angles formed by a line (the transversal) that cuts two parallel lines. The angles, one exterior and one interior, are on the same side of the transversal.

CORRESPONDING SIDES

Sides of similar figures that are proportional.

COSINE

The cosine of an acute angle of a triangle is the ratio of the length of the side adjacent to the angle of the hypotenuse.

CUBE

A rectangular prism whose six faces are squares.

CUBE of a number

The third power of a number; e.g., the cube of 2, written 2^3, is $2 \times 2 \times 2$ or 8.

CUBIC

Of the third degree; cubic equation; e.g.,
$$2x^3 + 3x^2 + 4 = 0$$

CYLINDER

A space figure that has two circular bases that are the same size and are in parallel planes. It has one curved face.

DECAGON

A polygon that has 10 sides.

DECIMAL

Any number written in decimal notation (a decimal point followed by one or more digits). Decimal points followed by one digit are tenths: 0.8 is read "8 tenths." Decimal points followed by two digits are hundredths: 0.05 is read "5 hundredths." Decimal points followed by three digits are thousandths: 0.123 is read "123 thousandths."

DEGREE

of a term: with one variable is the exponent of the variable; e.g., the term $2x^4$ is of the fourth degree.
of an equation: with one variable is the value of the highest exponent; e.g., $3x^3 + 5x^2 + 4x + 2 = 0$ is a third degree equation.

DEGREES

A unit of measure of angles or temperatures; e.g., there are 90 degrees in a right angle; today's temperature is 48 degrees.

DENOMINATOR

The term below the line in a fraction; e.g., the denominator of $\frac{2}{3}$ is 3.

DEPENDENT EQUATIONS

A system of equations in which every set of values that satisfies one of the equations satisfies them all; e.g.,

$$5x + 8y = 10$$
$$10x + 16y = 20$$

DEPENDENT VARIABLES

A variable whose values are considered to be determined by the values of another variable; $y + 2x + 3$; if $x = 4$ then $y = 11$, but if $x = 1$ then $y = 5$.

DESCENDING ORDER

From highest to lowest; the algebraic expression $5x^4 + x^3 - 2x^2 + 3x - 1$ is arranged in descending order of powers of x.

DIAGONAL

The line segment joining two non-adjacent vertices in a quadrilateral.

DIAMETER

Of a circle is a straight line passing through the center of the circle and terminating at two points on the circumference.

DIFFERENCE

The result of subtracting one quantity from another; 320 is the difference between 354 and 34.

DIRECT

Proof: Uses an argument that makes direct use of the hypotheses and arrives at a conclusion.
Variation: A relationship determined by the equation $y = kx$, where k is a constant.

DISTANCE

The length of the line joining two points or the length of a perpendicular line joining two lines. Distance may be expressed in inches, feet, yards, miles, etc.

DISTRIBUTIVE LAW

For any numbers replacing a, b, and c,

$$a(b + c) = ab + ac$$
$$2(3 + 5) = 2(3) + 2(5)$$
$$2(8) = 6 + 10$$
$$16 = 16$$

DIVIDEND

A quantity being divided in a division problem; e.g., $30 \div 5 = 6$ (30 is the dividend).

DIVISIBLE

The ability to be evenly divided by a number; e.g., 10 is divisible by 2 because $10 \div 2 = 5$.

DIVISOR

The quantity by which the dividend is being divided; e.g., $30 \div 5 = 6$ (5 is the divisor).

DOMAIN

The defined set of values the independent variable is assigned; e.g., in $y = x + 5$, x is the independent variable. If $x = \{0, 1\}$ is the domain, then $y = \{5, 6\}$.

EQUATION

A statement of equality between two expressions; e.g., $3 + x = 8$. The left-hand member $3 + x$ is equivalent to the right-hand member 8.
Literal equation: An equation containing variables as its terms.
Fractional equation: An equation with at least one term being a fraction.
Radical equation: An equation with at least one term being a square root.

EQUILATERAL

All sides are the same measure; e.g., an equilateral triangle contains three equal sides.

EQUIVALENT

Equations: Equations that have the same solution set; e.g., the equation $x + 6 = 10$ and $4x = 16$ are equivalent because 4 is the only solution for both.
Expressions: Expressions that represent the same value for any variable involved; e.g., $3x + 3y$ and $3(x + y)$.

EVALUATE

To find the value of; e.g., to evaluate $3 \times 2 + 4$ means to compute the result, which is 10; to evaluate $x^2 + x + 1$ for $x = 2$ means to replace x with 2; e.g.,

$$2^2 + 2 + 1 = 4 + 2 + 1 = 7$$

EVEN NUMBER

An integer that is divisible by 2. All even numbers can be written in the form $2n$, where n is any integer.

EXCLUSION

The act of leaving something out; e.g., write the set of all even numbers between 1 and 11. The solution set is {2, 4, 6, 8, 10}; the odd numbers from 1 to 11 are *excluded* from the solution set.

EXPONENT

A number placed at the right of and above a symbol. The number indicates how many times this symbol is used as a factor; e.g., in x^3, 3 is the exponent indicating that x is used as a factor three times. $x^3 = (x)(x)(x)$.

EXTERIOR ANGLE

Of a triangle is an angle formed by the one side of a triangle and the extension of the adjacent side.

FACTORIAL

For a positive integer n, the product of all the positive integers less than or equal to n. Factorial n is written $n!$

$$1! = 1$$
$$2! = (1)(2)$$
$$3! = (1)(2)(3)$$

FACTORING

The process of finding factors of a product. Types:
(a) greatest common factor
$$2x^2 + 2xy = 2x(x + y)$$
(b) difference between 2 squares
$$x^2 - 25 = (x - 5)(x + 5)$$
(c) factoring a trinomial
$$x^2 + 6x + 5 = (x + 1)(x + 5)$$
(d) factoring completely
$$5x^2 - 5 = 5(x^2 - 1) = 5(x - 1)(x + 1)$$

FACTORS

Any of a group of numbers that are multiplied together yielding the original given number; e.g., the positive factors of 12 are:

$$2 \text{ and } 6 \ (2 \times 6 = 12)$$
$$3 \text{ and } 4 \ (3 \times 4 = 12)$$
$$1 \text{ and } 12 \ (1 \times 12 = 12)$$

FORMULA

A special relationship between quantities expressed in symbolic form, an equation; e.g., area of a rectangle is length times width. The formula is $A = lw$.

FRACTIONS

A fraction is part of a whole. It is written $\frac{A}{B}$.

B is the denominator and tells how many parts the whole was divided into. A is the numerator and tells the number of equal parts used; e.g., in $\frac{3}{4}$ the whole is divided into 4 parts with 3 of the 4 being used.

GREATEST COMMON FACTOR (GCF)

The greatest integer that is a factor of both integers being considered; e.g., the GCF of 5 and 20 is 5.

HEXAGON

A polygon that has six sides.

HORIZONTAL

Parallel to level ground.

HUNDREDTHS

A decimal point followed by two digits; e.g., .27 is 27 hundredths and .09 is 9 hundredths.
See decimals

HYPOTENUSE

The side opposite the right angle in a right triangle. It is the longest side of the triangle.

IDENTITY

A statement of equality; any quantity is equal to itself; e.g.,

$$4 = 4$$
$$AB = AB$$
$$x + 6 = x + 6$$

Additive identity (0): a number that can be added to any quantity without changing the value of the quantity.
Multiplicative identity (1): a number that can be multiplied times any quantity without changing the value of the quantity.

IMPROPER FRACTION

A fraction whose numerator is equal to or greater than its denominator; e.g., $\frac{3}{3}, \frac{16}{7}, \frac{5}{4}$.

INCONSISTENT EQUATIONS

Equations that have no common solution set. Graphically they appear as parallel lines, since there would be no intersecting point; e.g.,

$$x + y = 8$$
$$x + y = 4$$

INDEPENDENT VARIABLE
A variable considered free to assume any one of a given set of values; e.g., in $y = 3x$, x can be any integer, and y is the dependent variable.

INEQUALITY
A statement that one quantity is less than (or greater than) another; not equal to ($\neq$); e.g.,

$A < B$ A is less than B
$A > B$ A is greater than B
$A \neq B$ A is not equal to B

INSCRIBED ANGLE
An angle whose sides are chords of a circle and whose vertex is a point on the circumference.

INSCRIBED CIRCLE
A circle within a polygon, the circle being tangent to every side of the polygon.

INTEGER
Any of the counting numbers, their additive inverses, and 0; e.g.,

1 { ... -4, -3, -2, -1, 0, 1, 2, 3, 4, ...}

INTERCEPT
To pass through a point on a line; x-intercept is the point on the x-axis where a line intersects it; y-intercept is the point on the y-axis where a line intersects it.

INTERSECTION
of two lines: is the point where they meet.
of two sets: consists of all the members that belong to both sets. The symbol used is "$\cap$"; e.g.,

Set A {2, 4, 6}
Set B {2, 3, 4}
$A \cap B$ {2, 4}

INVERSE
See additive inverse, multiplicative inverse
Variation: When the product of two variables is constant, one of them is said to *vary* inversely as the other. If $y = \dfrac{c}{x}$ or $xy = c$, y is said to vary inversely as x or x to vary inversely as y.

IRRATIONAL NUMBER
Any real number that is not the quotient of two integers; e.g., $\sqrt{2}$, $\sqrt{7}\pi$.

ISOSCELES TRAPEZOID
A trapezoid whose non-parallel sides are equal.

ISOSCELES TRIANGLE
A triangle with two equal sides.

LEGS
The sides of a right triangle adjacent to the right angle are called legs.

LIKE TERMS
Terms whose variables (letters) are the same; e.g., $3x$ and $12x$.

LINE SEGMENT
A part of a line that consists of two points on the line, called endpoints, and all the points between them.

LINEAR
Equation: An equation of the first degree. The graph of a linear equation in two variables is a straight line.

LITERAL EQUATION
An equation containing variables as its terms.

LOCUS
The set of all points, and only those points, that satisfy a given condition.

LOWEST COMMON DENOMINATOR (LCD)
The smallest natural number into which each of the denominators of a given set of fractions divide exactly, e.g., the LCD for $\dfrac{3}{4}$, $\dfrac{2}{3}$, and $\dfrac{1}{6}$ is 12.

MAJOR ARC
A major arc is an arc that is larger than a semi-circle; the larger arc formed by an inscribed or central angle in a circle.

MAXIMUM
The greatest value of an item; e.g., the maximum value of the sine of an angle is 1.

MINIMUM
The lowest value of an item.

MINOR ARC
An arc that is smaller than a semi-circle; the smaller arc formed by an inscribed or central angle of a circle.

MONOMIAL

An algebraic expression consisting of a single term; e.g.,

$$8x^2, 5xy$$

MULTIPLE

A number that is the product of a given integer and another integer; e.g., 12 is a multiple of 2, 3, 4, 6, or 12.

MULTIPLICATIVE INVERSE

When the product of two numbers is 1, one is called the reciprocal or multiplicative inverse of the other; e.g., $8\left(\dfrac{1}{8}\right) = 1$, therefore $\dfrac{1}{8}$ is the multiplicative inverse of 8 or 8 is the multiplicative inverse of $\dfrac{1}{8}$.

NET

Clear of all charges, cost, loss; e.g., net salary is salary after all deductions have been subtracted from the gross salary.

NUMERATOR

The expression above the line in a fraction. In the fraction $\dfrac{3}{4}$, 3 is the numerator.

OBTUSE

Obtuse angle is an angle greater than 90° and smaller than 180°. Obtuse triangle is a triangle, one of whose angles is obtuse.

OCTAGON

A polygon that has eight sides.

ODD

An odd number is a number that is not evenly divisible by 2; e.g., 1, 3, 5, 7, 9, …

OPEN SENTENCE

A sentence or equation that is neither true nor false; e.g., $x + 3 = 7$. If $x = 4$, the sentence is true; for all other values of x the sentence is false.

ORIGIN

The point on a line graph corresponding to zero. The point of intersection of the x-axis and y-axis. The coordinates of the origin are (0, 0).

ORDER OF OPERATIONS

In performing a series of operations, multiplication and division are performed before addition and subtraction in order from left to right.

ORDERED PAIR

An ordered pair (x, y) specifying the distance of points from two perpendicular number lines (x and y-axis); e.g., in (4, 6) the first number—the x number (4)—is called the *abscissa*. The second number—the y number (6)—is called the ordinate.

PARALLEL

Everywhere equally distant; parallel lines are two lines that never meet no matter how far they are extended. The symbol is ∥.

PARALLELOGRAM

A polygon with four sides and two pairs of parallel sides.

PENTAGON

A polygon that has five sides.

PERCENT(AGE)

Hundredths (symbol %); e.g., 5% of a quantity is $\dfrac{5}{100}$ of it.

PERFECT SQUARE

A perfect square is the exact square of another number; e.g., 4 is the perfect square of 2, since $2 \times 2 = 4$.

PERIMETER

The sum of the lengths of the side of a polygon; the distance around an area.

PERPENDICULAR

Perpendicular lines are lines that meet and form right angles (symbol ⊥).

Pi

The name of the Greek letter that corresponds to the letter P (symbol π). It represents the ratio of the circumference of a circle to its diameter. The equivalent value assigned is $\dfrac{22}{7}$, $3\dfrac{1}{7}$, or 3.14.

POINT
An undefined element of geometry; it has position but no non-zero dimensions.

POLYGON
A plane figure consisting of a certain number of sides. If the sides are equal, then the figure is referred to as regular. Examples are: triangle (3-sided); quadrilateral (4-sided); pentagon (5-sided); hexagon (6-sided); heptagon (7-sided); octagon (8-sided); nonagon (9-sided); decagon (10-sided); dodecagon (12-sided); n-gon (n-sided).

POLYNOMIAL
A special kind of algebraic expression usually used to describe expressions containing more than three terms: one term = monomial; two terms = binomial; three terms = trinomial; four or more = polynomial.

POSITIVE
Having a value greater than zero.

POWER
See exponent

PRIME FACTOR
A factor that is a prime number; e.g., 2, 3, and 5 are the prime factors of 30.

PRIME NUMBER
A natural number greater than 1 that can only be divided by itself and 1. A prime number has *no* factors other than itself and 1; e.g.,
$$2 = 2 \times 1$$
$$3 = 3 \times 1$$
$$5 = 5 \times 1$$

PRINCIPAL SQUARE ROOT
The positive square root of a number; e.g., the principal square root of 100 is 10.

PROBABILITY
The likelihood of something happening.

PRODUCT
The answer to a multiplication problem; e.g., the product of 8 and 5 is 40.

PROOF
The logical argument that establishes the truth of a statement.

PROPER FRACTION
A fraction whose numerator is smaller than its denominator; e.g., $\frac{1}{2}, \frac{3}{4}, \frac{7}{11}$.

PROPORTION
The equality of two ratios. Four numbers A, B, C, and D are in proportion when the ratio of the first pair $A:B$ equals the ratio of the second pair $C:D$. Usually written as $\frac{A}{B} = \frac{C}{D}$. A and D are the extremes and B and C are the means.

PYTHAGOREAN THEOREM
The sum of the squares of the lengths of the legs of a right triangle is equal to the square of the length of the hypotenuse. (Given sides a and b of a right triangle with hypotenuse c, then $a^2 + b^2 = c^2$.)

PYTHAGOREAN TRIPLES
Any set of numbers that satisfies the Pythagorean Theorem $a^2 + b^2 = c^2$; e.g., 3, 4, 5; 5, 12, 13; and 7, 24, 25 are Pythagorean triples.

QUADRANT
In the coordinate system, one of the four areas formed by the intersection of the x-axis and the y-axis.

QUADRATIC
Of the second degree; a quadratic equation is a polynomial equation of the second degree; e.g.,
$$x^2 + 3x + 5 = 0$$

QUADRILATERAL
A polygon that has four sides.

QUADRUPLED
Multiplied four times; e.g., $4x$ represents x quadrupled.

QUOTIENT
The quantity resulting from the division of two numbers; e.g., 2 is the quotient of 6 divided by 3.

RADICAL
A symbol ($\sqrt{}$) indicating the positive square root of a number; $\sqrt[3]{}$ indicates a cube root, $\sqrt[4]{}$ indicates a fourth root.

RADICAND

The quantity under a radical sign; e.g., 2 in $\sqrt{2}$, $a+b$ in $\sqrt{a+b}$.

RADIUS (RADII)

Line segment(s) joining the center of a circle and a point on the circumference.

RANGE

The set of values the function (y) takes on; e.g., $y = x + 5$; if the domain of $x = 0, 1$, then the range of y is 5, 6.

RATIO

The quotient of two numbers; e.g., ratio of 3 boys to 4 girls is 3 to 4, 3:4, or $\dfrac{3}{4}$.

RATIONAL NUMBER

A number that can be expressed as an integer or a quotient of integers; e.g., $\dfrac{1}{2}$, $\dfrac{4}{3}$, or 7.

REAL NUMBER

Any number that is a rational number or an irrational number.

RECIPROCAL

The reciprocal of a number is a number whose product with the given number is equal to 1. *See* multiplicative inverse.

RECTANGLE

A quadrilateral whose angles are right angles.

REDUCE

To lower the price of an item; to reduce a fraction to its lowest terms; e.g., $\dfrac{8}{10}$ becomes $\dfrac{4}{5}$.

REFLEXIVE

The reflexive property of equality; any number is equal to itself; e.g., $5 = 5$.

REMAINDER

When an integer is divided by an integer unevenly, the part left over is the remainder.

REMOTE (NON-ADJACENT) INTERIOR ANGLES of a triangle

The two angles that are *not* adjacent to an exterior angle of the triangle.

RHOMBUS

A parallelogram with adjacent sides equal.

RIGHT ANGLE

An angle containing 90°.

RIGHT TRIANGLE

A triangle that contains a right angle. The two perpendicular sides are called legs; and the longest side, which is opposite the right angle, is called the hypotenuse.

ROOT OF AN EQUATION

The solution; the value that makes the equation true; e.g., in $x + 5 = 15$, 10 is the root of the equation.

ROUND OFF

When the number to the right of the place being rounded off is 4, 3, 2, 1, or 0, the number stays the same; e.g., .54 rounded off to tenths becomes .5; .322 rounded off to hundredths becomes .33. When the number to the right of the place is 5, 6, 7, 8, or 9, the number being rounded off goes up 1; e.g., .55 to the tenths place becomes .6; .378 to the hundredths place becomes .38.

SCALENE

A scalene triangle is a triangle with no two sides equal.

SECANT OF A LINE

A secant is a line drawn from a point outside a circle, which intersects a circle in two points.

SECTOR

A portion of a circle bounded by two radii of the circle and one of the arcs they intercept.

SEGMENT

A part of a line; in a circle, the area between a chord and the arc being intercepted.

SEMI-CIRCLE

One-half of a circle; the two areas in a circle formed by drawing a diameter.

SIDES

A side of a polygon is any one of the line segments forming the polygon.

SIMILAR

terms: like terms; e.g., $5x^2$ and $8x^2$, $4x$ and $12x$.

triangles: two triangles are similar (symbol ~) if the angles of one equal the angles of the other and the corresponding sides are in proportion.

SIMPLIFY

To find an equivalent form for an expression that is simpler than the original.

SINE OF AN ANGLE

The sine of an acute angle of a triangle is the ratio of the length of the side opposite the angle over the hypotenuse.

SLOPE

The ratio of the change in y to the change in x; e.g., given A (x_1, y_1) and B (x_2, y_2), then slope equals

$$\frac{A}{B} = \frac{y_2 - y_1}{x_2 - x_1}$$

SPHERE

The set of all points in space at a given distance from a fixed point.

SQUARE (exponent)

The result of multiplying a quantity by itself; e.g., the square of 3 is 9; it is written $3^2 = 9$.

SQUARE (figure)

A four-sided figure with four right angles and four equal sides.

SQUARE ROOT

One of two equal factors of a number. Since (2)(2) = 4, the number 2 is the square root of 4. Also, since (-2)(-2) = 4, -2 is a square root of 4.

STRAIGHT ANGLE

An angle whose measure is 180°.

SUBSTITUTION

Replacing a quantity with another value; e.g., in $5x$ substituting 4 for x we have $5x = 5(4) = 20$.

SUPPLEMENTARY

angles: two angles whose sum is 180°, two angles whose sum is a straight angle. The angles are supplements of each other.

SYMMETRIC

The symmetric property of equality. An equality may be reversed; e.g., if 4 + 3 = 5 + 2, then 5 + 2 = 4 + 3.

TANGENT to a circle

A line that intersects a circle at one—and only one—point on the circumference.

TANGENT of an angle

The ratio of the length of the leg opposite the angle over the length of the leg adjacent to the angle.

TENTHS

Decimal point followed by one digit; e.g., 0.5 = five tenths.

THOUSANDTHS

Decimal point followed by three digits; e.g., 0.005 = 5 thousandths; 0.023 = 23 thousandths; 0.504 = 504 thousandths.

TRANSITIVE

Transitive property of equality states that. If one number is equal to the second number and the second number is equal to the third number, then the first number is also equal to the third number. If 5 + 4 = 6 + 3 and 6 + 3 = 7 + 2, then 5 + 4 = 7 + 2.

TRANSVERSAL

A line intersecting two or more lines in different points.

TRAPEZOID

A polygon with four sides and exactly one pair of parallel sides.

TRIANGLE

A polygon with three sides. *See* acute, obtuse, scalene, isosceles, right, and equilateral triangles.

TRINOMIAL

A polynomial of three terms; e.g.,
$$x^2 - 3x + 5$$

TRIPLED

Three times a quantity; e.g., x tripled = $3x$.

TRISECT

The process of separating into three equal parts.

UNION
Of sets A and B is the set containing all the elements of both set A and set B (symbol $\cup$); e.g., A = {1, 2, 3} and B = {2, 3, 4}, so A $\cup$ B = {1, 2, 3, 4}.

UNIT
A standard of measurement such as inches, feet, dollars, etc.

UNLIKE TERMS
Terms that differ in their variable factors; e.g., $23xy$ and $4x$, $3x^2$ and $3x^3$.

VARIABLE
A symbol representing any one of a given set of numbers. Most common are x and y.

VERTEX
of an isosceles triangle: the angle formed by the two equal sides;
of an angle: *See* angle.

VERTICAL
angles: two non-adjacent angles at a vertex formed when two lines intersect.
line: a line perpendicular to a horizontal line.

VERTICES
Of a triangle are the three points that form the triangle.

VOLUME
A number describing the three-dimensional extent of a set; e.g., Volume of a cube = length times width times height or $V = lwh$.

WHOLE NUMBER
A natural number or zero; one of the numbers {0, 1, 2, 3, …}.

WIDTH
Breadth of a plane figure; e.g., in a rectangle, the length of the shorter side.

YIELD
The percentage rate that gives a certain profit; e.g., yield on a bond is the amount of interest paid.

Summary of Formulas, Properties, and Laws

I. Properties of Integers

Commutative Laws of addition and multiplication
$$a + b = b + a$$
$$(a)(b) = (b)(a)$$

Associative Laws of addition and multiplication
$$(a + b) + c = a + (b + c)$$
$$(ab)c = a(bc)$$

Distributive Law $a(b + c) = ab + ac$

Binomial Expansion
$$(a + b)^2 = a^2 + 2ab + b^2$$

Sum of all consecutive odd integers beginning with $1 = n^2$

Sum of n consecutive integers $= \dfrac{n}{2}(a + l)$

n = number of terms
$a = 1^{st}$ term
l = last term

Average $= \dfrac{a + b + c}{n}$, where a, b, and c are terms and n is the number of terms.

II. Properties of Fractions

$$\frac{a}{b} + \frac{c}{d} = \frac{ad}{bd} + \frac{bc}{bd} = \frac{ad + bc}{bd}$$

$$\frac{a}{b} - \frac{c}{d} = \frac{ad - bc}{bd}$$

$$\frac{a}{b} \times \frac{c}{d} = \frac{ac}{bd}$$

$$\frac{a}{b} \div \frac{c}{d} = \frac{a}{b} \times \frac{d}{c} = \frac{ad}{bc}$$

III. Properties of a Proportion

If $\dfrac{a}{b} = \dfrac{c}{d}$ then $bc = ad$.

Product of the means equals the product of the extremes.

If $\dfrac{a}{b} = \dfrac{c}{d}$ then $\dfrac{a}{c} = \dfrac{b}{d}$ or $\dfrac{d}{b} = \dfrac{c}{a}$

The means and extremes may be interchanged without changing the proportion.

IV. Order of Operations

(1) All work inside parentheses
(2) All work involving powers
(3) All multiplication and division from left to right
(4) All addition and subtraction from left to right

V. Laws of Exponents

$$x^a + x^b = x^a + x^b$$
$$x^a - x^b = x^a - x^b$$
$$(x^a)(x^b) = x^{a+b}$$
$$\frac{x^a}{x^b} = x^{a+b}$$
$$(x^a)^b = x^{ab}$$
$$x^0 = 1$$
$$(xy)^a = x^a y^a$$
$$\left(\frac{x}{y}\right)^a = \frac{x^a}{y^a}$$
$$x^{\frac{a}{b}} = \sqrt[b]{x^a}$$

VI. Laws of Square Roots—A and B are Positive or Zero

$$\sqrt{a} + \sqrt{b} = \sqrt{a} + \sqrt{b}$$
$$\sqrt{a} - \sqrt{b} = \sqrt{a} - \sqrt{b}$$
$$\left(\sqrt{a}\right)\left(\sqrt{b}\right) = \sqrt{ab}$$
$$\frac{\sqrt{a}}{\sqrt{b}} = \sqrt{\frac{a}{b}}$$
$$\left(\sqrt{a}\right)^2 = \sqrt{a}\sqrt{a} = \sqrt{a^2} = a$$

VII. Some Commonly Used Percent, Decimal, and Fraction Equivalents

$16\frac{2}{3}\% = .167 = \frac{1}{6}$	$62\frac{1}{2}\% = .625 = \frac{5}{8}$
$33\frac{1}{3}\% = .333 = \frac{1}{3}$	$87\frac{1}{2}\% = .875 = \frac{7}{8}$
$66\frac{2}{3}\% = .667 = \frac{2}{3}$	$20\% = .2 = \frac{1}{5}$
$83\frac{1}{3}\% = .833 = \frac{5}{6}$	$40\% = .4 = \frac{2}{5}$
$12\frac{1}{2}\% = .125 = \frac{1}{8}$	$60\% = .6 = \frac{3}{5}$
$37\frac{1}{2}\% = .375 = \frac{3}{8}$	$80\% = .8 = \frac{4}{5}$

VIII. Some Commonly Used Squares

$7^2 = 49$	$14^2 = 196$
$8^2 = 64$	$15^2 = 225$
$9^2 = 81$	$16^2 = 256$
$10^2 = 100$	$17^2 = 289$
$11^2 = 121$	$18^2 = 324$
$12^2 = 144$	$19^2 = 361$
$13^2 = 169$	$25^2 = 625$

IX. Some Commonly Used Square Roots

$\sqrt{2} = 1.414$	$\sqrt{64} = 8$
$\sqrt{3} = 1.732$	$\sqrt{81} = 9$
$\sqrt{4} = 2$	$\sqrt{100} = 10$
$\sqrt{9} = 3$	$\sqrt{121} = 11$
$\sqrt{16} = 4$	$\sqrt{144} = 12$
$\sqrt{25} = 5$	$\sqrt{225} = 15$
$\sqrt{36} = 6$	$\sqrt{400} = 20$
$\sqrt{49} = 7$	$\sqrt{625} = 25$

X. Some Common Square Root Equivalents

$$\sqrt{12} = \sqrt{4}\sqrt{3} = 2\sqrt{3}$$
$$\sqrt{18} = \sqrt{9}\sqrt{2} = 3\sqrt{2}$$
$$\sqrt{24} = \sqrt{4}\sqrt{6} = 2\sqrt{6}$$
$$\sqrt{50} = \sqrt{25}\sqrt{2} = 5\sqrt{2}$$
$$\sqrt{48} = \sqrt{16}\sqrt{3} = 4\sqrt{3}$$
$$\sqrt{72} = \sqrt{36}\sqrt{2} = 6\sqrt{2}$$
$$\sqrt{96} = \sqrt{16}\sqrt{6} = 4\sqrt{6}$$
$$\sqrt{75} = \sqrt{25}\sqrt{3} = 5\sqrt{3}$$

XI. Formulas for Squares and Rectangles (Quadrilaterals)

1. Perimeter of square equals $4s$ (s is the length of one side).
2. Area of square equals s^2 or $\frac{d^2}{2}$ (where d is diagonal); Diagonal of square equals $\sqrt{2a}$ (a is area).
3. Perimeter of rectangle equals $2l + 2w$ (l is length, w is width).
4. Area of rectangle equals lw (length times width).
5. The four angles of any quadrilateral total 360 degrees.

XII. Formulas for Circles

1. Circumference of circle equals $2\pi r$ or πd ($\pi \approx \frac{22}{7}$ or 3.14).

2. Area of circle equals πr^2.

3. Radius of circle equals $\frac{C}{2\pi}$ (use when circumference is known).

4. Radius of circle equals $\sqrt{\frac{A}{\pi}}$ (use when area is known).

5. Entire circle is 360 degrees. Semi-circle is 180 degrees. Quarter circle is 90 degrees. Each hour of a clock is 30 degrees.

6. Length of an arc $= \frac{n}{360} \, 2\pi r$.

7. Area of sector $= \frac{n}{360} \, \pi r^2$.

8. Arc of circle/circumference $= \frac{n}{360}$.

XIII. Formulas for Triangles

1. Perimeter of any triangle is $a + b + c$ (sum of lengths of sides).

2. Perimeter of equilateral triangle is $3s$ (s is one side).

3. In a right triangle, $a^2 + b^2 = c^2$; $c = \sqrt{a^2 + b^2}$.

4. Right triangle combinations or ratios to watch for are: 3, 4, 5; 6, 8, 10; 9, 12, 15; 5, 12, 13; 8, 15, 17; and 7, 24, 25.

5. In a 30°-60°-90° right triangle, the ratio of the sides is $1 : 2 : \sqrt{3}$. Side opposite the 30° angle $= \frac{1}{2}$ hyp.

   Side opposite 60° angle $= \frac{1}{2}$ hyp $\sqrt{3}$. The larger leg equals the shorter leg times $\sqrt{3}$.

6. In a 45°-45°-90° right triangle, the ratio of the sides is $1 : 1 : \sqrt{2}$. Side opposite the 45° angle $= \frac{1}{2}$ hyp $\sqrt{2}$. Hypotenuse $= s\sqrt{2}$ where $s =$ a leg.

7. Area of a triangle equals $\frac{1}{2}(bh)$ (b is base, h is height).

8. Area of an equilateral triangle equals $\left(\frac{s}{2}\right)^2 \sqrt{3}$ (s is the length of one side).

9. There are 180 degrees in a triangle. There are 60 degrees in each angle of an equilateral triangle.

XIV. Formulas for Solids

1. Volume of cube is e^3 (e is one edge).

2. Volume of a rectangular solid is $l \times w \times h$.

3. Volume of a cylinder $= \pi r^2 h$ (area of a circular bottom times height).

4. Volume of a sphere equals $\frac{4}{3}\pi r^3$.

5. A cube has 6 faces, 8 vertices, and 12 edges.

6. Surface area of a sphere $= 4\pi r^2$.

7. Volume of a right triangular prism is $V = bh$ (b is the area of the base which is a triangle and h is the height).

8. Volume of a right circular cone is
$$V = \frac{1}{3}\pi r^2 h$$
(r is the radius of the circular base and h is the height of the cone).

XV. Facts About Angles

1. Number of degrees in any polygon is $(n-2)180$ (n is the number of sides).
2. Each angle of a regular polygon measures $\dfrac{(n-2)(180)}{n}$.
3. Vertical angles are congruent. Complementary angles total 90 degrees. Supplementary angles total 180 degrees.
4. An exterior angle equals the sum of the two non-adjacent interior angles.

XVI. Coordinate Geometry Formulas

Given points $= a(x_1, y_1)$ and $b(x_2, y_2)$.
Midpoint C having coordinates (x, y) is:

$$x = \frac{x_1 + x_2}{2} \quad y = \frac{y_1 + y_2}{2} .$$

Thus, midpoint C would have coordinates

$$\frac{x_1 + x_2}{2} \quad \frac{y_1 + y_2}{2} .$$

Distance from point A to point B is

$$\sqrt{(x_2 - x_1)^2 + (y_2 - y_1)^2} .$$

Slope of the line (m) passing through point A (x_1, y_1) and point B (x_2, y_2) is

$$m = \frac{y_2 - y_1}{x_2 - x_1} .$$

Slope—Intercept form is $y = mx + b$ where slope equals m and the y intercept is b.

XVII. Quadratic Formula

$ax^2 + bx + c = 0$

$$x = -b \pm \sqrt{\frac{b^2 - 4ac}{2a}}$$

PRACTICE TEST A

60 minutes – 60 questions

Directions: Answer each question. Choose the correct answer from the 5 choices given. Do not spend too much time on any one problem. Solve as many as you can; then return to the unanswered questions in the time left. Unless otherwise indicated, all of the following should be assumed:

- All numbers used are real numbers.
- The word *average* indicates the arithmetic mean.
- Drawings that accompany problems are intended to provide information useful in solving the problems. Illustrative figures may not be drawn to scale.
- The word *line* indicates a straight line.

---

1. $\dfrac{1}{3} - \dfrac{2}{15} + \dfrac{7}{25} = ?$

    A. $\dfrac{6}{25}$

    B. $\dfrac{12}{25}$

    C. $\dfrac{6}{43}$

    D. $\dfrac{9}{43}$

    E. $\dfrac{12}{43}$

DO YOUR FIGURING HERE.

---

2. A car traveled 882 miles on 36 gallons of gasoline. How many miles per gallon did the car get on this trip?

    F. 21.5
    G. 22.5
    H. 23.5
    J. 24.5
    K. 25.5

---

3. A yearly newspaper subscription price is $95.00. At the newsstand the paper costs $0.45 for each issue printed five days per week. How much money can be saved by purchasing the yearly subscription?

    A. $ 9.00
    B. $12.00
    C. $22.00
    D. $32.00
    E. $43.00

4. In the figure below, how many degrees is
    ∠*x*?

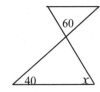

    F.   20°
    G.   40°
    H.   60°
    J.   80°
    K.   100°

---

5. If $4x - 3y = 10$, what is the value of
    $12x - 9y$?

    A. $3x$
    B. $3y$
    C.   10
    D.   20
    E.   30

---

6. If $\cos \alpha = \dfrac{3}{5}$ in the first quadrant, what does

    cot α equal?

    F. $\dfrac{3}{4}$

    G. $\dfrac{3}{5}$

    H. $\dfrac{4}{3}$

    J. $\dfrac{4}{5}$

    K. $\dfrac{5}{3}$

---

7. What is the positive value of $\sqrt{\dfrac{1}{25}}$ less

    0.20?

    A.   5
    B.   0.5
    C.   0.05
    D.   0.005
    E.   0

8. If the hypotenuse of isosceles right triangle ABC is $8\sqrt{2}$, what is the area of $\triangle ABC$?

   F. 8
   G. 16
   H. 32
   J. 64
   K. 128

9. It takes Mr. Smith H hours to mow his lawn. After three hours it begins to rain. How much of the lawn is not mowed?

   A. $H - 3$

   B. $\dfrac{H-3}{3}$

   C. $\dfrac{H}{3} - 1$

   D. $\dfrac{H-3}{H}$

   E. $3H$

10. Which of the following best describes the function graphed below?

   F. increasing at an increasing rate
   G. increasing at a decreasing rate
   H. decreasing at an increasing rate
   J. decreasing at a decreasing rate
   K. A relationship cannot be determined.

11. What is the quantity $\dfrac{7+7+7}{-7-7-7}$ equal to?

   A. $+1$
   B. -1
   C. $+21$
   D. -21
   E. -3

3

12. What do the graphs of $y = 6x + 7$ and $y = -2x + 7$ have what in common?

    F. They are parallel to each other.
    G. They are perpendicular to each other.
    H. They both pass through the point (6, -2).
    J. They both have the same x-intercept.
    K. They both have the same y-intercept.

13. In the sketch below, the area of each circle is 4π. What is the perimeter of $WXZY$?

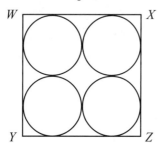

    A. 8
    B. 32
    C. 16π
    D. 64
    E. 4π

14. The graph of $y = x^3 + 3x^2 - 2x - 3$ crosses the x-axis in

    F. exactly two places
    G. one or two places
    H. two or three places
    J. one or three places
    K. A relationship cannot be determined.

15. In the coordinate plane, a square has vertices (4, 3), (-3, 3), (-3, - 4), and

    A. (4, -4)
    B. (3, 4)
    C. (0, 7)
    D. (4, 0)
    E. A relationship cannot be determined.

4

16. If $\csc \theta = \frac{4}{3}$, what is the value of $\sin \theta$?

    F. $1\frac{1}{3}$

    G. $\frac{3}{4}$

    H. $\frac{4}{3}$

    J. $\frac{3}{5}$

    K. 1

---

17. Which symbol below makes this expression true?
    $$2^4 \underline{\quad} 4^2$$

    A. $>$
    B. $=$
    C. $<$
    D. $+/-$
    E. A relationship cannot be determined.

---

18. If $a^2 - b^2 = 648$, and $(a - b) = 24$, what is the value of $(a + b)$?

    F. 21
    G. 24
    H. 25
    J. 26
    K. 27

---

19. Given trapezoid $ABCD$ with $\overline{AB} \parallel \overline{DC}$ and $AD = BC$, what is the measure of $\angle x$?

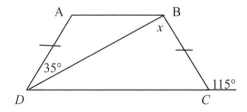

    A. 5
    B. 65
    C. 75
    D. 85
    E. 95

5

20. What is the ratio of the area of a circle with radius r to the circumference of a circle with radius $2r$?

    F. $2\pi : r$
    G. $r : 2\pi$
    H. $r : 4$
    J. $1 : 1$
    K. $4\pi : 2r$

21. The function $\begin{array}{|c|c|} \hline M & N \\ \hline O & P \\ \hline \end{array}$ is defined as

$MP - NO$. What is the value of $\begin{array}{|c|c|} \hline 2 & 4 \\ \hline 6 & 8 \\ \hline \end{array}$?

    A.   -8
    B.   -6
    C.   -4
    D.   -2
    E.   4

22. In a classroom survey of twelve students, it was determined that one-half of the students belong to the Chess Club, one-third belong to the Drama Club, and one-fourth belong to both clubs. How many students are not in either club?

    F.   4
    G.   5
    H.   6
    J.   7
    K.   13

23. For which value of x is the inequality $-2x \geq 6$ true?

    A.   -3
    B.   -2
    C.   -1
    D.   0
    E.   4

24. One billion minus one million = ?

    F.   10 million
    G.   99 million
    H.   100 million
    J.   101 million
    K.   999 million

_____

25. The houses on the odd side of Park Avenue
    are numbered consecutively. How many
    houses are there with an address less than
    1500 and greater than 1465?

    A.   14
    B.   15
    C.   16
    D.   17
    E.   18

_____

26. Given the sketch below, what is the value of
    $a + b + c + d$?

    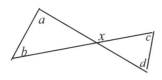

    F. x
    G. $2x$
    H. $180 - x$
    J. $180 - 2x$
    K. 90

_____

27. Assuming $a \neq 0$, what is the value of a in
    $\dfrac{(15)(16)}{a} = (3)(4)(5)$?

    A.   -4
    B.   0
    C.   4
    D.   31
    E.   60

28. If p and q are both positive integers and
$\dfrac{p-q}{5} = \dfrac{4}{10}$, which of the following is true?

    F. $p > q$
    G. $q > p$
    H. $p = q$
    J. $5p = 4q$
    K.   A relationship between p and q
            cannot be determined.

29. City A is 200 miles east of City C. City B is 150 miles directly north of City C. What is the shortest distance (in miles) between City A and City B?

    A.   200
    B.   250
    C.   300
    D.   350
    E.   400

30. The relation $\overset{\triangle}{R}$ is defined as $\overset{\triangle}{R} = R^2 - 1$. $\overset{\triangle}{8} = ?$

    F.   7
    G.   21
    H.   63
    J.   64
    K.   512

31. A 24-inch diameter pizza is cut into eight slices. What is the area of one slice?

    A. 3π
    B. 6π
    C. 12π
    D. 18π
    E. $\dfrac{\pi}{8}$

32. The perimeter of a rectangle is 26 units. Which of the following cannot be dimensions of the rectangle?

    F.   1 and 12
    G.   4 and 9
    H.   8 and 5
    J   10 and 6
    K.   11 and 2

33. M is the midpoint of line segment RS. If $\overline{RM} = 3x + 1$ and $\overline{RS} = 38$, what is the value of x?

    A.   6
    B.   12
    C.   18
    D.   19
    E.   21

34. Assuming $x \neq 0$, how can the expression $(3x)^2 + 6x^0 + (5x)^0$ be simplified?

    F. $3x^2 + 11$
    G $9x^2 + 7$
    H. $3x^2 + 6$
    J. $9x^2 + 11$
    K. $6x^2 + 5$

35. Which of the following triples cannot be the lengths of the sides of a triangle?

    A.   1, 2, 3
    B.   4, 5, 6
    C.   7, 8, 9
    D.   10, 11, 12
    E.   13, 14, 15

36. How many two-digit numbers have a remainder of 2 when divided by 10 and also have a remainder of 2 when divided by 4?

    F.   2
    G.   4
    H.   6
    J.   8
    K.   infinitely many

37. In the figure below, *ABCDEF* is a hexagon and $m \angle BCD = 72°$. What is the ratio of $m \angle BCD$ to the sum of the interior angles of *ABCDEF* ?

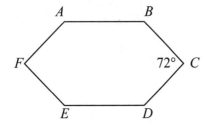

    A.   1 : 4
    B.   1 : 6
    C.   1 : 8
    D.   1 : 10
    E.   1 : 12

---

38. Given that *r* varies directly as the square of *d*, and $r = 48$ when $d = 4$, what is the value of *r* when $d = 20$?

    F.   240
    G.   400
    H.   1,200
    J.   1,240
    K.   1,440

---

39. Roger is a baseball player who gets a hit about $\frac{1}{3}$ of the times he comes to bat. Last year he batted 636 times. Assuming he had no "walks," how many outs did he make?

    A.   202
    B.   212
    C.   221
    D.   424
    E.   633

40. What is the slope of the line perpendicular to a line with the equation $ax + by = c$?

    F. $\dfrac{b}{a}$

    G. $-\dfrac{b}{a}$

    H. $\dfrac{c}{a}$

    J. $-\dfrac{a}{b}$

    K. $b^2 - 4ac$

---

41. If $(x - y) = 15$, what is the value of $x^2 - 2xy + y^2$?

    A. 25
    B. 30
    C. 125
    D. 225
    E. 625

---

42. A woman has two rectangular gardens. The larger garden is five times as wide and three times as long as the smaller one. If the area of the smaller one is x, what is the difference in size of the two gardens?

    F. $5x$
    G. $7x$
    H. $14x$
    J. $15x$
    K. $20x$

---

43. If $b^4 - 5 = 226$, what is the value of $b^4 + 9$?

    A. 240
    B. 235
    C. 231
    D. 221
    E. 212

44. If the radius of a circle is reduced by 50 percent, by what percent is its area reduced?

    F. $33\frac{1}{3}\%$

    G.   50%

    H. $66\frac{2}{3}\%$

    J.   75%

    K.   80%

---

45. If $12x = 216$, what is the value of $\frac{x}{9}$?

    A.   2
    B.   6
    C.   12
    D.   18
    E.   81

---

46. What is the value of cos B in the sketch below?

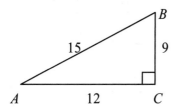

    F. $\frac{2}{5}$

    G. $\frac{3}{5}$

    H. $\frac{4}{5}$

    J. $\frac{5}{3}$

    K. $\frac{5}{4}$

47. Given circle O with minor arc $\overset{\frown}{AB} = 60°$ and $OA = 12$. What is the area of sector AOB ?

DO YOUR FIGURING HERE.

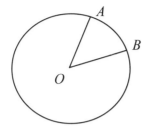

    A. 12π
    B. 24π
    C. 36π
    D. 72π
    E. 720π

---

48. If both a and b are negative, what is the value of $a - b$?

    F.   positive
    G.   negative
    H.   zero
    J.   one
    K.   A relationship cannot be determined.

---

49. If $3^{n+1} = 81$, what is the value of n ?

    A.   1
    B.   2
    C.   3
    D.   4
    E.   5

---

50. A man walks d miles in t hours. At that rate, how many hours will it take him to walk m miles?

    F. $\dfrac{mt}{d}$

    G. $\dfrac{d}{t}$

    H. $\dfrac{md}{t}$

    J. $\dfrac{dt}{m}$

    K. dtm

51. Which of the following has the greatest number of integer factors other than itself and one?

    A. 12
    B. 16
    C. 24
    D. 27
    E. 29

52. Paterson Pond was stocked with 2,000 fish, all bass and trout. The ratio of bass to trout was 3 : 2. How many of each type were put in the pond?

    F. 800 bass and 1,200 trout
    G. 1,200 bass and 800 trout
    H. 600 bass and 1,400 trout
    J. 800 bass and 1,000 trout
    K. 300 bass and 200 trout

53. A computer program generates a list of triples (a, b, c) such that

    > a is an even number less than 16,
    > b is a perfect square, and
    > c is a multiple of 5 between a and b.

    Which of the following triples does not meet those conditions?

    A. (14, 36, 25)
    B. (10, 25, 20)
    C. (6, 64, 50)
    D. (2, 25, 15)
    E. (2, 16, 12)

54. If $(y + 2)(5y - 2) = 0$ and $y > 0$, what is the value of y ?

    F. 2
    G. $\frac{5}{2}$
    H. $\frac{2}{5}$
    J. 0
    K. -2

14

55. Given the sketch below, which of the following statements about rectangle *ABDC* is true?

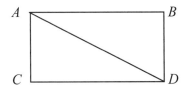

    A. $AB + BD > AD$
    B. $AB + BD < AD$
    C. $AB + BD = AD$
    D. $(AB)(BD) = AD$
    E.   A relationship cannot be determined.

56. Given: $4a + 5b - 6 = 0$ and $4a - 2b + 8 = 0$, what is the value of *b* ?

    F.   -2
    G. $-\dfrac{1}{2}$
    H.   0
    J. $\dfrac{1}{2}$
    K.   2

57. If the ordered pair (5, 4) is reflected across the *y*-axis and then reflected across the *x*-axis, what are the new coordinates of that point?

    A.   (-5, -4)
    B.   (-5, 4)
    C.   (-4, -5)
    D.   (5, -4)
    E.   (4, 5)

58. A 45-rpm record revolves 45 times per minute. Through how many degrees will a point on the edge of the record move in 2 seconds?

    F.   180
    G.   360
    H.   540
    J.   720
    K.   930

59. If $|x + 8| = 12$, what is the value of x ?

    A.   4 only
    B.   20 only
    C.   either -20 or 4
    D.   either -4 or 20
    E.   either 0 or 12

---

60. Which of the following has the same result as reducing an item in price using successive discounts of 30% and 20%?

    F.   multiplying the original price by 56%
    G.   dividing the original price by 50%
    H.   multiplying the original price by 44%
    J.   dividing the original price by 44%
    K.   either multiplying the original price by 50% or by 30% and then 20%

END OF PRACTICE TEST A

PRACTICE TEST B

60 minutes – 60 questions

Directions: Answer each question. Choose the correct answer from the 5 choices given. Do not spend too much time on any one problem. Solve as many as you can; then return to the unanswered questions in the time left. Unless otherwise indicated, all of the following should be assumed:

- All numbers used are real numbers.
- The word *average* indicates the arithmetic mean.
- Drawings that accompany problems are intended to provide information useful in solving the problems. Illustrative figures are not necessarily drawn to scale.
- The word *line* indicates a straight line.

DO YOUR FIGURING HERE.

1. In one city the taxicabs charge $2.50 for the first mile and $0.75 for each additional $\frac{1}{8}$ of a mile. What is the cost of a $3\frac{1}{4}$ mile trip?

    A. $13.50
    B. $14.50
    C. $16.00
    D. $18.00
    E. $26.00

2. $\left(\frac{1}{3}\right)^4 - \left(\frac{1}{3}\right)^3 = ?$

    F. $\frac{1}{3}$

    G. $\frac{1}{9}$

    H. $\frac{1}{81}$

    J. $-\frac{2}{81}$

    K. $-\frac{1}{3}$

3. In the figure $l_1 \parallel l_2$ and l_3 is a transversal. What is the value of $q - p$?

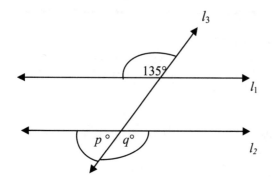

A. $0°$
B. $45°$
C. $55°$
D. $60°$
E. $90°$

4. Six calculators cost $\$x$. What is the cost of y less calculators?

F. $\dfrac{6-x}{y}$

G. $\dfrac{y-6}{x}$

H. $\dfrac{x-6}{6y}$

J. $\dfrac{x(6-y)}{6}$

K. $6x(y-6)$

5. Jean bought a used car for $\$2,800$ plus 6% tax. How much more would she have paid for the car if the sales tax were 7% instead of 6%?

A. $\$ 28$
B. $\$ 56$
C. $\$168$
D. $\$196$
E. $\$336$

18

6. If $\tan x = \frac{3}{4}$, what is the value of $\cos x + \sin x$?

   F. $\frac{4}{3}$

   G. $\frac{9}{16}$

   H. $\frac{7}{5}$

   J. $\frac{25}{12}$

   K. 1

7. A square sheet of metal with sides $4a$ has a circle of diameter $2a$ and a rectangle of length $2a$ and width a removed from it. What is the area of remaining metal?

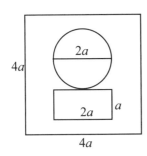

   A. $4a - 4\pi a^2 - 2a^2$
   B. $14a^2 - \pi a^2$
   C. $14a^2 - 4\pi a^2$
   D. $4a^2 + \pi a^2 - a$
   E. $4a^2 - 2\pi a^2$

8. Which of the following equations has a graph that is a line perpendicular to the graph of $x + 2y = 6$?

   F. $2x - y = 3$
   G. $2x + y = -3$
   H. $x - 2y = 3$
   J. $y + x = 3$
   K. $2y + x = -3$

9. If $x = ut + \frac{1}{2}at^2$, what is t when $x = 16$, $u = 0$, and $a = 4$?

   A. $2\sqrt{2}$
   B. $4\sqrt{2}$
   C. $\sqrt{2}$
   D. 2
   E. 4

DO YOUR FIGURING HERE.

10. If 18% of the senior class of 200 students were absent from school, how many students were present?

    F. 38
    G. 120
    H. 136
    J. 164
    K. 182

11. What is the area between the square and circle shown?

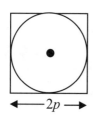

    $\longleftarrow 2p \longrightarrow$

    A. $4p^2(1 - \pi)$
    B. $p^2(4 - 2\pi)$
    C. $4p^2(1 + \pi)$
    D. $p^2(4 - \pi)$
    E. $p^2(\pi - 4)$

12. The points A, B, C, and D divide the line segment AD in the ratio $4 : 3 : 1$, respectively, and $AB = 24$ cm. What is the length of BD ?

    F. 12 cm
    G. 14 cm
    H. 18 cm
    J. 19 cm
    K. 24 cm

20

13. $\dfrac{2a-3}{2} - \dfrac{5a+3}{5} = ?$

   A. -21

   B. -9

   C. $-\dfrac{21}{10}$

   D. $-\dfrac{9}{10}$

   E. $\dfrac{9}{10}$

14. A plumber charges $35 flat fee plus $25 per hour. If his bill was $147.50, how long did the job take?

   F. $1\dfrac{1}{2}$

   G. $1\dfrac{3}{4}$

   H. $2\dfrac{1}{4}$

   J. $3\dfrac{1}{2}$

   K. $4\dfrac{1}{2}$

15. If $a = 1$, what is the value of $[(a+3)^2 - (a-3)^2]^2$?

   A.   10
   B.   12
   C.   24
   D.   120
   E.   144

16. If the area of the triangle is 8, what is the value of x ?

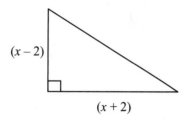

$(x-2)$

$(x+2)$

   F. $5\sqrt{2}$
   G. $2\sqrt{5}$
   H. $4\sqrt{3}$
   J. $2\sqrt{3}$
   K. $3\sqrt{2}$

17. $2\sqrt{24} - 2\sqrt{2} \times \sqrt{3} = ?$

   A. 0
   B. $3\sqrt{24}$
   C. -6
   D. $2\sqrt{6}$
   E. $4\sqrt{6}$

18. Vijay saves 20% on a $125 bowling ball but must pay 6% sales tax. What is the total he must pay?

   F. $ 94.00
   G. $100.00
   H. $106.00
   J. $107.50
   K. $205.00

19. The average (mean) temperature for five days was 2°. If the temperatures for the first four days were -10°, 30°, 0° and -5°, what was the temperature on the fifth day?

   A. -10°
   B. - 5°
   C. 0°
   D. 5°
   E. 20°

20. $\frac{2}{17} \div \frac{-4}{34} \div \frac{-1}{2} = ?$

   F.   2

   G. $\frac{1}{2}$

   H.   0

   J. $-\frac{1}{2}$

   K.   -2

21. If $(x + 2)^2 = (2^2)^3$ and $x > 0$, what is the value of x ?

   A.   2
   B.   3
   C.   4
   D.   6
   E.   -10

22. Solve $x^2 + 3x + 2 = 0$.

   F.   {-2, -3}
   G.   {-2, 3}
   H.   {-1, -2}
   J.   {-1, 2}
   K.   {1, 2}

23. If the endpoints of the diameter of a circle in the x–y plane have coordinates $\left(-\sqrt{2}, \sqrt{\frac{3}{2}}\right)$ and $\left(\sqrt{2}, -\sqrt{\frac{3}{2}}\right)$, what are the coordinates of the center?

   A. $(2\sqrt{2}, -\sqrt{3})$
   B. $(2, -\frac{3}{4})$
   C. $(0, 0)$
   D. $(\sqrt{3}, -\sqrt{3})$
   E. $(-2, -\frac{3}{4})$

24. What is the equation of the line, in standard form, connecting points (2, -3) and (4, 4)?

    F. $7x - 2y - 26 = 0$
    G. $7x + y - 13 = 0$
    H. $7x - 2y - 20 = 0$
    J. $2x - 2y - 7 = 0$
    K. $3x - y + 10 = 0$

---

25. If quadrilateral *ABCD* is a parallelogram with an area of 180 square units and a base of 20 units, what is its height?

    A. 9
    B. 5
    C. 4
    D. $3\frac{1}{2}$
    E. $1\frac{1}{4}$

---

26. $0.25 \div \left(\dfrac{1}{4} \div \dfrac{25}{100} \right) = ?$

    F. $\dfrac{1}{16}$
    G. $\dfrac{1}{4}$
    H. 1
    J. 4
    K. 16

---

27. If $x + y = 4$ and $2x - y = 5$, what is the value of $x + 2y$?

    A. 1
    B. 2
    C. 4
    D. 5
    E. 6

28. If $5x + 3y = 23$ and x and y are positive integers, which of the following can be equal to y ?

    F.   3
    G.   4
    H.   5
    J.   6
    K.   7

29. Which equation could be used to find the unknown, if $\frac{1}{2}$ less than $\frac{3}{5}$ of a number is the same as the number?

    A. $\frac{1}{2} - \frac{3}{5}x = \frac{1}{2}$

    B. $\frac{1}{2} - \frac{3}{5}x = r$

    C. $x - \frac{1}{2} = \frac{3}{5}x$

    D. $\frac{3}{5}x - \frac{1}{2} = x$

    E. $\frac{1}{2} - x = \frac{3}{5}x$

30. If $x*$ means $4(x - 2)^2$, what is the value of $(3*)*$?

    F.   8
    G.   12
    H.   16
    J.   36
    K.   None of the above

31. What is the vertex of the parabola $y = (x + 3)^2 - 6$?

    A.   (3, 6)
    B.   (-3, 6)
    C.   (3, -6)
    D.   (-3, -6)
    E.   None of the above

32. What is the slope of the line connecting the points (2, -2) and (3, -2)?

    F.   undefined
    G.   1
    H.   0
    J.   -1
    K.   -4

33. Which of the following is not equal to the other four?

    A. 1.1×10
    B.   110%
    C. $\sqrt{1.21}$
    D. $\dfrac{11}{10}$
    E. $1 + \dfrac{1}{10}$

34. According to the diagram, which of the following statements is true?

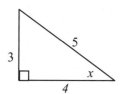

    F $\sin x = \dfrac{5}{3}$

    G. $\cos x = \dfrac{3}{5}$

    H. $\tan x = \dfrac{5}{4}$

    J. $\cos x = \dfrac{4}{5}$

    K. $\sin x = \dfrac{4}{5}$

35. If △*ABE* is similar to △*ACD*, what is the value of *AB* ?

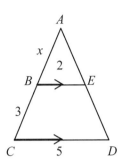

A. $7\frac{1}{2}$

B. 3

C. 2

D. $1\frac{1}{2}$

E. -2

36. What is the probability of selecting a letter M or T, if the letters M, A, T, H, E, M, A, T, I, C, and S are drawn randomly from a bag?

F. $\frac{4}{11}$

G. $\frac{3}{11}$

H. $\frac{2}{11}$

J. $\frac{1}{11}$

K. 0

37. A salesman is paid $150/week plus *x*% commission on all sales. If he had $*s* in sales, what was the amount of his paycheck (*p*)?

A. $p = 150 + \frac{xs}{10}$

B. $p = 150 + s$

C. $p = 150 + 0.01xs$

D. $p = 150 + xs$

E. $p = 150 + 100xs$

27

38. If $2 + \dfrac{x}{(x-2)} = 4$, what is the value of

$-|x|$?

    F.   -4
    G.   -2
    H.   0
    J.   2
    K.   4

39. Which of the following lines is parallel
to $2y = 3x - 1$?

    A. $y = \frac{1}{3}x - 1$
    B. $2y = x - 3$
    C. $4y = 6x + 8$
    D. $y = 3x + 4$
    E. $3y = 2x - 3$

40. Given $\triangle ABC$ with $AB = 4$ and $m \angle ACD$
= 135°, what is the value of AC ?

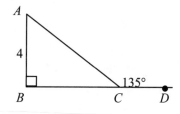

    F.   4
    G. $4\sqrt{2}$
    H. $3\sqrt{2}$
    J.   8
    K.   5

41. If the diameter of a bicycle wheel is 50
centimeters, how many revolutions will
the wheel make to cover a distance of
100π meters?

    A.   12
    B.   20
    C.   120
    D.   200
    E.   1200

42. If $x* = x + 2$, what is the value of $(3* + 5*)*$?

    F.　　8
    G.　　10
    H.　　12
    J.　　14
    K.　　None of the above

43. If $\dfrac{15k}{3kx+16} = 1$ and $x = 4$, what is the value of k?

    A.　　2
    B.　　3
    C.　　4
    D.　　8
    E.　　$\dfrac{16}{3}$

44. $-7 - 3 \times 2(-5) + 6 - 21 \div 3 = ?$

    F.　　99
    G.　　95
    H.　　33
    J.　　25
    K.　　22

45. Simplify $\dfrac{3y}{10} + \dfrac{7y-2}{5}$.

    A.　　$\dfrac{17y-4}{10}$

    B.　　$\dfrac{10y-2}{15}$

    C.　　$\dfrac{4y-2}{10}$

    D.　　$\dfrac{85y-2}{50}$

    E.　　$\dfrac{10y-2}{5}$

46. Which of the following is equivalent to

$$\frac{\cos x}{\sin x} + \frac{\sin x}{\cos x} \, ?$$

    F. $\dfrac{\cos x + \sin x}{\sin x \cos x}$

    G. $\dfrac{1}{\sin x \cos x}$

    H. $\tan x + \cos^2 x$

    J. $\sin x \cos x$

    K. $2 \sin x \cos x$

---

47. (-2, -3) is a solution to which inequality?

    A. $2y \geq 3x + 1$
    B. $-2y \leq -x + 3$
    C. $\dfrac{x}{2} \geq 4 - y$
    D. $y - 2 \geq (x - 3)$
    E. $x - y < 0$

---

48. What is the distance between the points (-3, 4) and (9, 9)?

    F.   5
    G. $5\sqrt{2}$
    H.   12
    J.   13
    K.   17

---

49. If the area of the semicircular region is 8π, what is the perimeter of the shape?

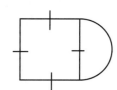

    A. $16 + 8\pi$
    B. $24 + 4\pi$
    C. $12 + 8\pi$
    D. $24 + 4\pi^2$
    E. $16 + 4\pi^2$

50. If $f(x) = x^2 - 5$ and $g(x) = 5x$, what is the value of $f(g(3)) - g(f(3))$?

    F. 400
    G. 240
    H. 200
    J.   40
    K.   0

---

51. What is the length of arc AB ?

    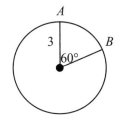

    A. π
    B. 2π
    C. 2.5π
    D. 3π
    E. 6π

---

52. If two sides of a triangle are 6 cm and 8 cm, which of these could be the third side?

    F.   1
    G.   2
    H.   7
    J. 14
    K. 15

---

53. If $x = 4$ is a solution of the equation $x^2 + kx - 24 = 0$, what is the value of k ?

    A. -6
    B. -2
    C.   2
    D.   4
    E.   6

31

54. Which of the following is not a solution for $|5 - 2x| \geq 3$?

    F.   -2
    G.   -1
    H.   0
    J.   2
    K.   5

---

55. Which of the following forms an identity with $\dfrac{\tan x}{\sec x}$?

    A. $\sin x$

    B. $\dfrac{\sin x}{\cos^2 x}$

    C. $\dfrac{\sin^2 x}{\cos x}$

    D. $\cot x$

    E. $\dfrac{1}{\sin x}$

---

56. $\dfrac{7}{2 - \sqrt{3}} = ?$

    F. $14 + 7\sqrt{3}$

    G. $-7\sqrt{3}$

    H. $21\sqrt{3}$

    J. $\dfrac{14 - 7\sqrt{3}}{-5}$

    K. $14\sqrt{3} - 5$

---

57. The roots of $2x^2 + 13x + 18 = 0$ are which of the following?

    I.   rational
    II. irrational
    III. imaginary

    A.   I only
    B.   II only
    C.   I and II only
    D.   II and III only
    E.   I, II, and III

58. $8^{\frac{2}{3}} \bullet 2^{-1} = ?$

    F. $\frac{1}{16}$

    G. $\frac{1}{2}$

    H.   2

    J.   4

    K.   16

---

59. If *ABCD* is a square and CDE is an equilateral triangle, what is the value of *x* ?

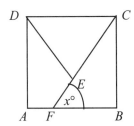

    A.   30°

    B.   40°

    C.   45°

    D.   50°

    E.   60°

---

60. In the figure below, $l_1 \parallel l_2$ and *t* is a transversal. What is the value of *x*?

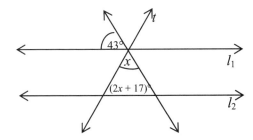

    F.   40°

    G.   42.5°

    H.   43°

    J.   46.5°

    K.   60°

END OF PRACTICE TEST B

PRACTICE TEST C

60 minutes – 60 questions

Directions: Answer each question. Choose the correct answer from the 5 choices given. Do not spend too much time on any one problem. Solve as many as you can; then return to the unanswered questions in the time left. Unless otherwise indicated, all of the following should be assumed:

- All numbers used are real numbers.
- The word *average* indicates the arithmetic mean.
- Drawings that accompany problems are intended to provide information useful in solving the problems. Illustrative figures are not necessarily drawn to scale.
- The word *line* indicates a straight line.

---

1. A mechanic charges $60 to determine what repairs are needed to a car and $45 per hour to repair the car. If the repairs on your car take three hours, what would your total bill be?

    A. $150
    B. $175
    C. $185
    D. $195
    E. $250

DO YOUR FIGURING HERE.

2. On average, 5 oranges yield 3 cups of juice. If 2 cups make one pint, how many oranges are needed to make 3 quarts of orange juice?

    F. 10
    G. 12
    H. 15
    J. 18
    K. 20

3. A is west of B and east of C.
    D is southwest of B and southeast of C.
    E is northwest of C.
    Which point is farthest west?

    A. D
    B. C
    C. B
    D. E
    E. A relationship cannot be determined.

4. What is the amplitude of the equation
   $y = 3 \sin 4x$?

   F. $4x$
   G. 4
   H. 3
   J. $3x$
   K. $\dfrac{x}{2}$

5. $1 + \dfrac{1}{1 + \dfrac{1}{1+1}} = ?$

   A. $\dfrac{2}{3}$
   B. $1\dfrac{2}{3}$
   C. $2\dfrac{1}{3}$
   D. $2\dfrac{2}{3}$
   E. $3\dfrac{1}{2}$

6. Given trapezoid *KLMN* below, what is
   the length of *KN* if the area of *KLMN* is
   54 square units?

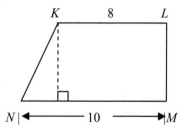

   F. 20
   G. 27
   H. 30
   J. $2\sqrt{10}$
   K. $10\sqrt{2}$

7. The ordered pair (-4, 0) lies in which quadrant?

    A. IV
    B. III
    C. II
    D. I
    E. none of the above

DO YOUR FIGURING HERE.

8. If $f(x) = 5$ and $g(x) = 5x$, what is the value of $g(x) - f(x)$?

    F. $g(5)$
    G. $f(5)$
    H. $g(x - 1)$
    J. $f(2x)$
    K. None of the above

9. If m men can move 50 boxes in one day, how many men will be needed to move x boxes in one day?

    A. $\dfrac{x}{50m}$
    B. $\dfrac{mx}{50}$
    C. $\dfrac{1}{50m}$
    D. $\dfrac{50x}{m}$
    E. $\dfrac{50m}{x}$

10. Which of the following is true about any cube?

    F. It has more vertices than edges.
    G. It has more faces than vertices.
    H. The number of vertices plus faces is greater than the number of edges.
    J. The number of edges plus faces equals the number of vertices.
    K. It has two more faces than vertices.

11. If $3x + 9y = 18$, what is the value of x ?

    A. $18 - 9y$
    B. $3y + 6$
    C. $6y + 3$
    D. $-3y + 6$
    E. $-6y + 3$

---

12. If $g^2 - g - 6 = 0$ and $g < 0$, what is the value of $-3g$?

    F. -6
    G. -3
    H. -2
    J. $-\dfrac{2}{3}$
    K. 6

---

13. What is the equation of the line perpendicular to $y = -2x + 5$ and passing through the point $(0, -2)$?

    A. $y = 2x - 2$
    B. $y = \dfrac{1}{2}x - 2$
    C. $y = -\dfrac{1}{2}x - 2$
    D. $y = -2x - 2$
    E. $y = -2x + 5$

---

14. $8[-6 + 5(10 - 12) + (18 - 3) \div 5] = ?$

    F. -104
    G. -13
    H. 13
    J. 104
    K. 117

38

15. A buyer paid $30 for an item. She wants to sell it at a 10% discount and still make a 20% profit. What price should she mark on the tag?

    A. $32.40
    B. $40.00
    C. $44.00
    D. $47.50
    E. $50.00

---

16. $4(x-8) - (2x+7) = ?$

    F. $2x - 25$
    G. $4x + 25$
    H. $2x + 25$
    J. $4x - 39$
    K. $2x - 39$

---

17. A box contains 8 red balls, 5 brown balls, 4 purple balls, and 3 green balls. What is the probability that a purple ball will be selected from the box after a red ball is taken out and not replaced?

    A. $\dfrac{1}{5}$

    B. $\dfrac{3}{5}$

    C. $\dfrac{3}{10}$

    D. $\dfrac{4}{19}$

    E. $\dfrac{4}{20}$

18. The figure below shows two parallel lines, l_1 and l_2, cut by transversal t. What is measure of angle x ?

DO YOUR FIGURING HERE.

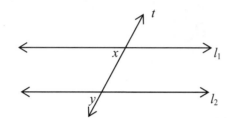

F. $2y$
G. $180 - y$
H. $180 - x$
J. y
K.   A relationship cannot be determined.

---

19. If $\dfrac{3k}{k+2} = 6$, what is the value of $|k|$?

A.   -4
B.   -2
C.   1
D.   2
E.   4

---

20. A pole casts a 6-foot shadow. If the distance from the top of the pole to the tip of the shadow is 10 feet, how tall is the pole?

F.   4
G.   8
H.   12
J.   16
K.   20

---

21. 8,328 is evenly divisible by which of the following?

A.   2, 3, 4, and 5
B.   2, 4, 5, and 6
C.   2, 3, 4, 7, and 8
D.   3, 4, 5, 6, and 7
E.   2, 3, 4, 6, and 8

22. In a certain high school, 30% of the students are on the honor roll, and 40% of the students are boys. If 15% of the students not on the honor roll are boys, then what percent of the girls are on the honor roll?

    F.   5%
    G.   15%
    H.   25%
    J.   55%
    K.   A relationship cannot be determined.

---

23. In circle O below, what is the area of the sector AOB if the $m \ \overset{\frown}{AB} = 30°$

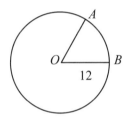

    A. 8π
    B. 10π
    C. 12π
    D. 15π
    E. 20π

---

24. Four students have different heights.
    The shortest is 60 inches.
    The tallest is 74 inches.
    Their average height is 68 inches.
    Which of the following cannot be the heights of the students (in inches)?

    F.   60, 67, 71, and 74
    G.   60, 65, 73, and 74
    H.   60, 68, 70, and 74
    J.   60, 64, 73, and 74
    K.   60, 66, 72, and 74

25. If $3(x + 2) = 5(x - 8)$, what is the value of $x + 2$?

    A.   23
    B.   25
    C.   40
    D.   46
    E.   50

---

26. Let $\{y\}$ be defined as $-y^2 - 6$. What is the value of $\{5\}$?

    F.   31
    G.   21
    H.   19
    J.   -21
    K.   -31

---

27. Which symbol makes this expression a true statement?

$$\frac{1}{9} + \frac{1}{16} \quad \underline{\quad\quad} \quad \frac{1}{16} + \frac{1}{9}$$

    A. $>$
    B. $<$
    C. $=$
    D. $+/-$
    E.   A relationship cannot be determined.

---

28. Which formula expresses the relationship between x and y in the table below?

x	1	2	3	4	5
y	-1	2	5	8	11

    F. $y = x + 5$
    G. $y = 2x - 4$
    H. $y = -2x + 4$
    J. $y = 3x - 4$
    K. $y = -3x - 4$

29. If $x \neq 0$, $x^2 = y$, and $2y = x$, what is the value of x ?

    A.   1

    B. $\dfrac{1}{2}$

    C. $\dfrac{1}{4}$

    D. $\dfrac{1}{8}$

    E. $\dfrac{1}{16}$

---

30. If $4x^2 - 7x + 10 = 0$, what is the sum of the roots divided by the product of the roots?

    F. $\dfrac{7}{4}$

    G. $\dfrac{5}{2}$

    H. $\dfrac{10}{7}$

    J. $\dfrac{2}{5}$

    K $\dfrac{7}{10}$

---

31. For how many integer values of x is $|x - 3| < 2$ a true statement?

    A.   0
    B.   2
    C.   3
    D.   4
    E.   5

32. If twice a number increased by 5 equals $\frac{3}{5}$, what is the number?

    F. $-\frac{5}{11}$

    G. $\frac{11}{5}$

    H. $\frac{5}{11}$

    J. $-\frac{11}{5}$

    K.   2

---

33. $\dfrac{\sin 60° \cos 30°}{\tan 45°} = ?$

    A.   0

    B. $\frac{1}{2}$

    C. $\frac{3}{4}$

    D. $\frac{4}{3}$

    E.   2

---

34. In the circle XY is a diameter. If the measure of $\angle ZXY$ is $a°$ and the measure of arc XZ is $b°$, what is the value of b ?

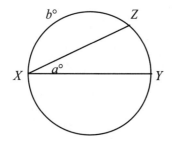

    F. $b = 180 - 2a$

    G. $b = 2a$

    H. $b = \dfrac{180 - a}{2}$

    J. $b = 180 - \dfrac{a}{2}$

    K. $b = 2(180 - a)$

35. How much should Kelly score on her third test to get an average of 91, if her previous scores are $x + 88$ and $90 - x$?

    A.   80
    B.   88
    C.   95
    D.   96
    E.   100

---

36. If $f(x) = \dfrac{x}{x-2}$, what is the value of $f(f(3))$?

    F.   -3
    G.   -1
    H.   0
    J.   1
    K.   3

---

37. $\left| 1 - \dfrac{1}{\left|1 + \dfrac{1}{2}\right|} \right| = ?$

    A.   3
    B. $\dfrac{3}{2}$
    C. $\dfrac{1}{3}$
    D. $-\dfrac{1}{3}$
    E.   -3

---

38. In the triangle below, what is the value of x?

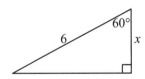

    F. $\sqrt{3}$
    G.   1
    H.   2
    J.   3
    K. $2\sqrt{3}$

39. In the figure below, what is the value of $x - b$?

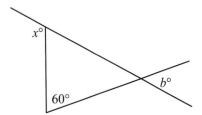

A. 60°
B. 65°
C. 70°
D. 75°
E. 85°

40. What is the ratio of the area of a circle with radius r to the circumference of the same circle?

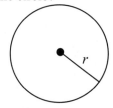

F. $2\pi r : 3$
G. $\pi^2 : 2$
H. $\pi r : 2$
J. $2\pi : r$
K. $r : 2$

41. If the radius of a circle is increased by 10%, by what percent is the area increased?

A. 10%
B. 20%
C. 21%
D. 32%
E. 100%

42. What is the product of the GCF of 4 and
6 and the LCM of 4 and 6?

    F.   4
    G.   6
    H.   12
    J.   24
    K.   28

DO YOUR FIGURING HERE.

43. In the figure below, $l_1 \parallel l_2$ with
transversal t. What is the value of x ?

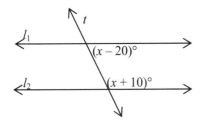

    A.   50
    B.   75
    C.   85
    D.   95
    E.   185

44. If $\sqrt{\left(x^2 + 7\right)} - 2 = x - 1$, what is the
value of x ?

    F.   -3
    G. $-\dfrac{1}{3}$
    H. $\dfrac{1}{3}$
    J.   3
    K.   A relationship cannot be determined.

45. In which of the following equations does
the product of the roots equal 14?

    A. $x^2 - 2x + 14 = 0$
    B. $2x^2 + x + 7 = 0$
    C. $x^2 + 14x + 5 = 0$
    D. $14x^2 + 2x + 1 = 0$
    E. $-2x^2 + 28x - 13 = 0$

46. The figure shows a circle with center O and a square $ABCO$. The shaded area represents what fraction of the square?

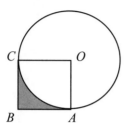

   F. $\dfrac{4 - \pi}{4}$

   G. $\dfrac{1}{4}$

   H. $\dfrac{\pi}{8}$

   J. $\dfrac{2\pi - 3}{3}$

   K.   A relationship cannot be determined.

47. The equation $x^3 - 3x^2 - 28x = 0$ has how many real roots?

   A.   0
   B.   1
   C.   2
   D.   3
   E.   4

48. In the circle $\overline{DE}$ is a diameter and $EF = OE$. What is the measure of arc DF ?

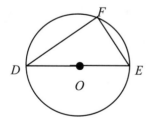

   F.   100°
   G.   120°
   H.   130°
   J.   150°
   K.   210°

49. What are the coordinates of the vertex of the parabola $y = -(x + 4)^2 - 2$?

    A. (2, 4)
    B. (-4, -2)
    C. (4, -2)
    D. (2, -4)
    E. (-2, -4)

---

50. Where does the graph of $y = x^2 - x - 20$ cross the x-axis?

    F. (5, 0) and (-4, 0)
    G. (10, 0) and (-2, 0)
    H. (4, 0) and (5, 0)
    J. (-5, 0) and (4, 0)
    K. (2, 0) and (-10, 10)

---

51. At 3 o'clock the hour hand of a clock points to the number 3. 120 minutes later, the hour hand has moved how many degrees to the number 5?

    A. 720°
    B. 360°
    C. 60°
    D. 45°
    E. 30°

---

52. What is the simplest form of
$$\frac{\sqrt{48}}{4} + 6\sqrt{\frac{1}{12}} - \sqrt{27} \text{ ?}$$

    F. $-2\sqrt{3} + 2\sqrt{2}$
    G. $4\sqrt{2}$
    H. $-\sqrt{3}$
    J. $2\sqrt{3}$
    K. 0

53. In the triangle below, side x is $\frac{3}{5}$ of side z. If side y is $\frac{4}{3}$ of side x, what is the ratio of y to z ?

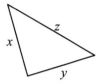

    A. $5 : 3$
    B. $5 : 4$
    C. $4 : 5$
    D. $3 : 4$
    E. $4 : 15$

---

54. What is the solution of $|2x - 1| = 7$?

    F. $\{0, 2\}$
    G. $\{1, 4\}$
    H. $\{2, -3\}$
    J. $\{-4, 3\}$
    K. $\{4, -3\}$

---

55. Simplify $(1 - \sin x)(1 + \sin x)$.

    A. $\sin x$
    B. $\cos^2 x$
    C. $\tan x$
    D. 1
    E. $\sin^2 x - 1$

---

56. If $2x^{-\frac{2}{5}} = 1$, what is the value of x ?

    F. $5\sqrt{3}$
    G. $2\sqrt{2}$
    H. $4\sqrt{2}$
    J. $5\sqrt{2}$
    K. $2\sqrt{3}$

57. What is the center of the circle
$2x^2 + 2y^2 - 4x + 16y = 128$?

    A.   (1, -2)
    B.   (1, 4)
    C.   (1, -4)
    D.   (-1, -2)
    E.   (-1, -4)

58. What is the amplitude of $f(x) = -2 \sin 5x$?

    F.   5
    G.   2
    H. $\frac{5}{2\pi}$
    J.   -2
    K.   -5

59. In the figure below, what is the length of
AB ?

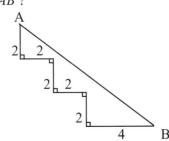

    A.   10
    B.   12
    C.   14
    D.   15
    E.   20

60. In the figure below, $l_1 \parallel l_2$ with
transversal t and $x = y = r$. What is the
value of r ?

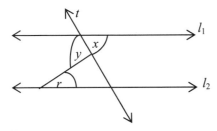

    F. $r = x + y$
    G. $r = y - x$
    H. $r = x - y$
    J. $r = 180 - x - y$
    K. $r = 2x + 2y$

END OF PRACTICE TEST C

If a numerical expression does not contain parentheses, first perform all multiplications and divisions, in order from left to right. Then perform all additions and subtractions, in order from left to right.

Example

What is the value of $6 - 5 \times 4 + 6 \div 3 + 4$?

Solution

Do the multiplications and divisions first, to give:

$$6 - 20 + 2 + 4$$

Then do the additions, left to right:

$$-14 + 2 + 4$$
$$-12 + 4$$
$$-8$$

If a numerical expression contains parentheses or brackets, roots, or powers, the order of operations is as follows. Perform all work within the parentheses/brackets first. Start with the innermost parentheses/brackets and work outward.

Example

What is the value of $[7 + (3 \times 5)]$?

Solution

Simplify the parentheses and then add:
$$[7 + 15]$$
$$22$$

Example

Simplify $\sqrt{6(2) - (9 - 1)}$.

Solution

(Parentheses first) $\sqrt{12 - 8}$
(Then subtract) $\sqrt{4}$
(Simplify the root)   2

Multiplication and Division of Fractions

When you multiply fractions, the denominators need not be the same. Simply multiply the numerators, multiply the denominators, and reduce the resulting fractions to lowest terms. Mixed numbers can be converted to improper fractions. Canceling common factors can make the problem easier and allow you to do less reducing of your final answer. Whole numbers can be converted to fractions by placing them over the number 1.

Example

$$1\frac{3}{8} \times 1\frac{1}{3} = ?$$

Solution

Change to improper fractions and multiply:

$$\frac{11}{8} \times \frac{4}{3} = \frac{11}{\underset{2}{8}} \times \frac{\overset{1}{4}}{3} = \frac{11 \times 1}{2 \times 3} = \frac{11}{6} = 1\frac{5}{6}$$

When dividing fractions, you do *not* need a common denominator. The easiest way to divide fractions is to change the division problem to a multiplication problem and then perform the same steps you would in multiplying fractions. To accomplish this conversion, find the reciprocal of the fraction you are dividing by and then multiply. An easier way to think of this is simply "invert" or turn the fraction you are dividing by upside down.

Example

$$3\frac{2}{3} \div 1\frac{1}{6} = ?$$

Solution

Change to improper fractions and multiply by the reciprocal of the divisor:

$$\frac{11}{3} \div \frac{7}{6} = \frac{11}{3} \times \frac{6}{7} =$$

$$= \frac{11}{3} \times \frac{\overset{2}{\cancel{6}}}{7} = \frac{11 \times 2}{1 \times 7} = \frac{22}{7} = 3\frac{1}{7}$$

Fractions, Decimals, and Percents

It is sometimes necessary to change a fraction to a decimal fraction. To do this, divide the numerator by the denominator, adding zeros after the decimal point in the numerator when they are needed.

Example

What is the decimal equivalent of $\frac{9}{20}$?

Solution

$$20\overline{)9.00}^{.45} \quad \text{Therefore } \frac{9}{20} = .45$$

Example

What is the decimal equivalent of $\frac{5}{8}$?

Solution

$$8\overline{)5.000}^{.625} \quad \text{Therefore } \frac{5}{8} = .625$$

To express a decimal as a percent, "move" the decimal point 2 places to the right and write the % sign.

Example

What is the percent equivalent of .35?

Solution

.35 = .35 = 35%

Example

What is the percent equivalent of .375?

Solution

.357 = .375 = 37.5%

Linear Equations with One Variable

There are standard methods of solving equations. The object in solving an equation is to isolate the variable on one side of the equation, keeping the original equation and the new equation equivalent.

Example

If $5x + 2 = 17$, then $x = ?$

Solution

Subtract 2 from both sides:

$$5x + 2 - 2 = 17 - 2$$
$$5x = 15$$

Divide both sides by 5:

$$\frac{5x}{5} = \frac{15}{5}$$
$$x = 3$$

Example

If $\frac{2}{3}y - 4 = \text{-}5$, then $y = ?$

Solution

Add 4 to both sides:

$$\frac{2}{3}y - 4 + 4 = \text{-}5 + 4$$

$$\frac{2}{3}y = \text{-}1$$

Multiply both sides by $\frac{3}{2}$:

$$\frac{3}{2} \times \frac{2}{3}y = \text{-}1 \times \frac{3}{2}$$

$$y = \text{-}\frac{3}{2}$$

Example

If $3x + 7 = 17 - 2x$, then $x = ?$

Solution

To collect all variables on the left side of the equation, add $2x$ to both sides:

$$3x + 2x + 7 = 17 - 2x + 2x$$
$$5x + 7 = 17$$

Subtract 7 from both sides:

$$5x + 7 - 7 = 17 - 7$$
$$5x = 10$$

Divide both sides by 5:

$$\frac{5x}{5} = \frac{10}{5}$$
$$x = 2$$

Example
If $3a + 1 + 2a = 6$, then $a = ?$

Solution
Combine like terms: $5a + 1 = 6$
Subtract 1 from both sides:
$$5a + 1 - 1 = 6 - 1$$
$$5a = 5$$
Divide both sides by 5:

$$\frac{5a}{5} = \frac{5}{5}$$
$$a = 1$$

Example
If $3(x + 5) = 51$, then $x = ?$

Solution
Remove the parentheses (distributive law):
$$3x + 15 = 51$$

Subtract 15 from both sides:
$$3x + 15 - 15 = 51 - 15$$
$$3x = 36$$

Divide both sides by 3:

$$\frac{3x}{3} = \frac{36}{3}$$
$$x = 12$$

Orientation Exercises

1. $\dfrac{14}{2} + 3(4 - 2) = ?$

    A. 12
    B. 13
    C. 17
    D. 20
    E. 38

2. $2\dfrac{2}{3} \times 1\dfrac{1}{3} = ?$

    A. $2\dfrac{2}{9}$

    B. $3\dfrac{5}{9}$

    C. $2\dfrac{1}{3}$

    D. $2\dfrac{5}{6}$

    E. 3

3. What is the decimal equivalent of $\dfrac{11}{20}$?

    A. 0.055
    B. 1.8
    C. 0.55
    D. 0.11
    E. 5.5

4. If $3x - 2 + 4x = 5$, then $x = ?$

    A. 3
    B. -3
    C. 7
    D. 1
    E. -1

Practice Exercises

1. $[2 + (3 \times 2)] = ?$

    A. 7
    B. 8
    C. 10
    D. 12
    E. 18

2. $16 + 20 \div 4 - 2 \times 2 = ?$

    A. 5
    B. 10
    C. 14
    D. 17
    E. 38

3. $\dfrac{5}{6} + \dfrac{5}{8} \times \dfrac{2}{3} = ?$

    A. $\dfrac{5}{9}$
    B. $\dfrac{10}{21}$
    C. $\dfrac{35}{36}$
    D. $1\dfrac{1}{4}$
    E. None of the above

4. $\dfrac{\frac{1}{2} + \frac{1}{5}}{\frac{1}{4}} = ?$

    A. $\dfrac{1}{14}$
    B. $\dfrac{3}{11}$
    C. $\dfrac{7}{40}$
    D. $1\dfrac{1}{7}$
    E. $2\dfrac{4}{5}$

5. What is the percent equivalent of .06?

    A. .006%
    B. .06%
    C. .6%
    D. 6%
    E. 60%

6. What is the decimal equivalent of $\dfrac{1}{12}$?

    A. $.08\overline{3}$
    B. $.008\overline{3}$
    C. .12
    D. .012
    E. None of the above

7. If $7x + 6 = 27$, then $x = ?$

    A. 2
    B. 3
    C. 9
    D. 13
    E. 21

8. If $3(y + 2) = 2(y + 4)$, then $y = ?$

    A. $\dfrac{1}{2}$
    B. 1
    C. 2
    D. 4
    E. 8

Practice Test

1. $12 + 24 \div 6 \times 3 = ?$

    A 2
    B. 9
    C. 18
    D. 24
    E. 48

2. $[4 + (3 - 1)]^3 = ?$

    A. 12
    B. 32
    C. 64
    D. 128
    E. 216

3. $1\dfrac{3}{4} \times 4\dfrac{2}{3} = ?$

    A. $2\dfrac{2}{3}$

    B. $4\dfrac{1}{2}$

    C. $4\dfrac{5}{7}$

    D. $8\dfrac{1}{6}$

    E. None of the above

4. $\dfrac{\frac{3}{10} - \frac{1}{5}}{\frac{2}{5} + 3} = ?$

    A. $\dfrac{1}{5}$

    B. $\dfrac{34}{5}$

    C. $\dfrac{1}{34}$

    D. $\dfrac{17}{5}$

    E. $\dfrac{17}{50}$

5. What is the percent equivalent of 0.2184?

    A. 0.002184%
    B. 0.02184%
    C. 0.2184%
    D. 2.184%
    E. 21.84%

6. What is the decimal equivalent of $\dfrac{7}{8}$?

    A. 0.08
    B. 0.8
    C. 0.78
    D. 0.875
    E. 0.078

7. If $\dfrac{3x}{2} - 4 - \dfrac{x}{2} = 1$, then $x = ?$

    A. $\dfrac{1}{4}$

    B. 1
    C. 2
    D. 4
    E. 5

8. If $9k - 3 = 3k + 15$, then $k = ?$

    A. 1
    B. 2
    C. 3
    D. 4
    E. 5

SKILL BUILDER TWO

Averages

Example
John got a 75 on his first math test, 85 on his second, 80 on his third, and 88 on his fourth. What was his average grade on the 4 tests?

Solution
To compute the average of a series of numbers, first add the numbers. Then divide the sum by the total number of numbers added. In the example, the 4 test grades are added: $75 + 85 + 80 + 88 = 328$. Then divide the sum by the number of grades, 4, to compute the average: $328 \div 4 = 82$.

It is possible to use a known average to compute one of the values that made up that average.

To do this, multiply the number of values or items by their average cost or average value to get the total value. Then subtract the sum of the known values from the total to obtain the remaining value.

Example
The average of 4 temperature readings is $1,572°$. Three of the actual readings are $1,425°$, $1,583°$, and $1,626°$. What is the fourth reading?

Solution
Multiply the average ($1,572°$) by the number of readings (4).

$$\begin{array}{r} 1,572° \\ \times \quad 4 \\ \hline 6,288° \end{array}$$

Add the 3 given readings.
$1,425° + 1,583° + 1,626° = 4,634°$.
Subtract this sum (4,634) from $6,288°$.

$$\begin{array}{r} 6,288° \\ -4,634° \\ \hline 1,654° \end{array}$$

Probability

Look for the total number of possible occurrences. Then look for the number of occurrences that did or will take place.

The probability of a favorable result occurring may be computed by dividing the number of favorable results by the number of possible results if they are all equally likely.

Example
There are 5 cherry, 7 orange, and 4 grape lollipops in a box. If you pick a lollipop from the box without looking, what is the probability that it will be orange or grape?

Solution
$$\frac{\text{Number of Favorable Outcomes}}{\text{Total Number of Possible Outcomes}}$$

$$\frac{7 \text{ orange} + 4 \text{ grape}}{(\text{Total})16} = \frac{7 + 4}{16} = \frac{11}{16}$$

Percentage Problems

Example
James bought a notebook for $1.25, a pen for $0.99, and a calculator for $9.99. Including a sales tax of 6%, what was the total bill, rounded to the nearest penny?

Solution
To solve a problem involving sales tax, first find the total price. To find the sales tax on the total price, change the percent sales tax to a decimal by moving the decimal point in the number 2 places to the left. Next multiply the decimal by the total price to give the sales tax. Add the sales tax to the total price to find the total bill.

Total price: $1.25
                         .99
                   + 9.99
                   $12.23

Change 6% to .06.

Multiply the decimal by the total price to get the sales tax:

$$\begin{array}{r} \$12.23 \\ \times .06 \\ \hline \$.7338 \end{array}$$

or $0.73, when it is rounded off.

Add the sales tax to the total price to find the total bill:

$$\begin{array}{r} \$12.23 \\ + 0.73 \\ \hline \$12.96 \end{array}$$

Example

The price of a certain stock rose from $60 a share to $65 a share. What was the percent of increase?

Solution

To find the percent of increase, form the fraction:

$$\frac{\text{Amount of Increase}}{\text{Original Amount}}$$

$$\frac{65-60}{60} = \frac{5}{60} = \frac{1}{12}$$

$$1 \div 12 = 0.08\frac{1}{3} = 8\frac{1}{3}\%$$

Example

During the past 5 years the student enrollment at the local high school decreased from 1,250 to 1,000. What was the percent of decrease?

Solution

Form a fraction showing the *decrease* over the original enrollment.

$$\frac{1,250-1,000}{1,250} = \frac{250}{1,250} = \frac{1}{5} \qquad 5\overline{)1.00}^{.20} = 20\%$$

Word Problems Containing Fractions

Example

Jim completed $\frac{2}{5}$ of a job. The next day he completed $\frac{5}{8}$ of the remaining part of the job. What fractional part of the original job is left?

Solution

Jim completed $\frac{2}{5}$ of the job, so $\frac{3}{5}$ of the job remains. Then he completed $\frac{5}{8}$ of the remaining part of the job, or

$$\frac{5}{8} \times \frac{3}{5} = \frac{\cancel{5}^{1}}{8} \times \frac{3}{\cancel{5}_{1}} = \frac{3}{8}$$

Since Jim completed $\frac{2}{5}$ of the job the first day and $\frac{3}{8}$ of the job the next day,

$$\frac{2}{5} + \frac{3}{8} = \frac{16}{40} + \frac{15}{40} = \frac{31}{40}$$

of the original job was completed. The amount of the original job that is left is

$$1 - \frac{31}{40} \text{ or } \frac{9}{40}$$

Word Problems Involving Money

Example

A local delivery service charges $1.80 for the first $\frac{2}{5}$ mile, $1.50 for the next $\frac{3}{5}$ mile, and $1.20 per mile thereafter. What is the cost to deliver a parcel to a company that is 5 miles away?

Solution

Cost for first $\frac{2}{5}$ mile = $1.80.

Cost for next $\frac{3}{5}$ mile = $1.50.

Since $\frac{2}{5} + \frac{3}{5} = \frac{5}{5}$ or 1 mile,

the cost of the first mile =

$$\begin{aligned} &\$1.80 \\ +\ &1.50 \\ \hline &\$3.30 \end{aligned}$$

The trip is 5 miles; therefore, the 4 additional miles cost

$$4 \times \$1.20 = \$4.80$$
$$\text{Total cost} = \$3.30 + \$4.80 = \$8.10$$

Word Problems Involving Proportions

A ratio is a comparison of numbers by division. A proportion is a statement that 2 ratios are equal.

Example
If Sarah can type 4 pages in 12 minutes, how long will it take her to type a 16-page report, working at the same rate?

Solution
To solve a problem involving proportions, set up a ratio that describes a rate or compares the first 2 terms. In the example, setting up a ratio with the first 2 terms gives:

$$\frac{4 \text{ pages}}{12 \text{ min.}}$$

Next, set up a second ratio that compares the third term and the missing term. Letting x stand for the missing term, the second ratio is:

$$\frac{16 \text{ pages}}{x \text{ min.}}$$

To solve for the missing term, set up a proportion where the ratios are equal:

$$\frac{4 \text{ pages}}{12 \text{ min.}} = \frac{16 \text{ pages}}{x \text{ min.}}$$

You may solve the proportion by cross multiplication.

$$\frac{4}{12} \diagdown\!\!\!\!\diagup \frac{16}{x}$$

$$4x = 12 \bullet 16$$
$$4x = 192$$
$$x = 48$$

Sarah can type the report in 48 minutes.

Orientation Exercises

1. The average height of 5 basketball players at South High School is 6 feet 2 inches. If four of these players have heights of 5' 8", 6' 0", 6' 5", and 6' 6", how tall is the fifth player?

   A. 5'10"
   B. 5'11"
   C. 6'1"
   D. 6'2"
   E. 6'3"

2. There are 6 blue, 8 green, 5 red, and 10 yellow marbles in a bag. If a marble is picked from the bag at random, what is the probability that it will be green or red?

   A. $\dfrac{1}{2}$

   B. $\dfrac{14}{29}$

   C. $\dfrac{13}{29}$

   D. $\dfrac{2}{14}$

   E. $\dfrac{1}{2}$

3. Wendy bought a wallet for $16.99, a key case for $10.95, and a duffel bag for $15.99. Including a sales tax of 5%, what was the total bill?
   A. $36.13
   B. $41.73
   C. $43.93
   D. $46.13
   E. $48.23

4. When the bus fare increased from 50¢ to 60¢, it represented a percent increase of

   A. 10%
   B. $16\dfrac{2}{3}\%$
   C. 20%
   D. 30%
   E. $83\dfrac{1}{3}\%$

5. During a sale of computers, one-fourth of the inventory was sold the first day. The next day two-thirds of the remaining inventory was sold. What percent of the total inventory was sold during the second day?

   A. $8\dfrac{1}{3}\%$

   B. $16\dfrac{2}{3}\%$

   C. 25%

   D. 50%

   E. $66\dfrac{2}{3}\%$

6. A long distance telephone call from Center City to Smithville costs $3.25 for the first 3 minutes and $0.45 for each additional minute. How many minutes can a person talk if the cost of the call is to be $10.00?

   A. 15
   B. 16
   C. 17
   D. 18
   E. 19

7. Charles earns $98 in 2 days. At the same rate of pay, how much will he earn in 5 days?

   A. $196
   B. $235
   C. $245
   D. $294
   E. None of the above

8. The Lane family drove 150 miles in 3 hours. Traveling at the same speed, how long will it take them to go an additional 250 miles?

   A. 4 hours
   B. 5 hours
   C. $5\dfrac{1}{2}$ hours
   D. 6 hours
   E. 8 hours

60

Practice Exercises

1. The video store rented 42 videotapes on Monday, 35 on Tuesday, 51 on Wednesday, and 32 on Thursday. What was the average number of videotapes initially rented per day from Monday to Thursday if all were one-day rentals?
   A. 37
   B. 38
   C. 40
   D. 44
   E. 54

2. In the tournament, the Tigers scored 44, 56, and 47 points in the first three games. If their four-game tournament average score was 52 points, how much did they score in their final game?
   A. 52
   B. 55
   C. 58
   D. 61
   E. None of the above

3. A box contains 150 balloons. There are 75 green balloons, 50 silver balloons, and 25 gold balloons. If you picked a balloon from the box at random, what is the probability that you would pick a silver balloon?
   A. $\frac{1}{6}$
   B. $\frac{1}{3}$
   C. $\frac{2}{3}$
   D. $\frac{3}{4}$
   E. $\frac{3}{5}$

4. Sandy has 13 rolls of ribbon on the top shelf of her closet: 8 rolls are red, 3 are yellow, and 2 are blue. If she picks a roll at random, what is the probability that it will be yellow or blue?
   A. $\frac{1}{2}$
   B. $\frac{5}{8}$
   C. $\frac{5}{13}$
   D. $\frac{2}{3}$
   E. None of the above

5. Tim bought a shirt for $10.99, a tie for $9.99, and a jacket for $59.00. Including a sales tax of 6%, what was the total bill?
   A. $68.74
   B. $74.68
   C. $78.48
   D. $79.98
   E. $84.78

6. Bill purchased six 6-packs of cola for $2.75 each. How much will this purchase cost including a 6% sales tax?
   A. $16.50
   B. $16.56
   C. $17.49
   D. $17.75
   E. $17.86

7. The price of cabbage increased from $0.16 a pound (in season) to $0.40 a pound (out of season). What was the percent of increase?
   A. 125%
   B. 140%
   C. 150%
   D. 200%
   E. 250%

8. The temperature dropped from 50° to 46°. What was the percent of decrease?
   A. 4%
   B. 8%
   C. 9%
   D. 10%
   E. None of the above

9. Mr. King left $\frac{1}{2}$ of his estate to his wife and $\frac{1}{3}$ of the remainder to his granddaughter. What part of his estate is not accounted for in this statement?
   A. $\frac{1}{3}$
   B. $\frac{1}{4}$
   C. $\frac{1}{5}$
   D. $\frac{1}{6}$
   E. $\frac{1}{8}$

10. Which of the following has the largest value?
    A. $\frac{1}{.05}$
    B. $\frac{1}{.5}$
    C. $\frac{.1}{5}$
    D. $\frac{.1}{.5}$
    E. .5

11. Karen worked five hours each day from June 15 through June 19. If she makes $5 per hour, how much did she earn?
    A. $100
    B. $115
    C. $125
    D. $135
    E. $140

12. Chris earns $65.00 a week delivering flowers for a local florist. In addition, he is paid $0.15 per mile for the use of his car. One week he traveled 156 miles making deliveries. How much was he paid that week?
    A. $ 23.40
    B. $ 66.50
    C. $ 88.40
    D. $124.80
    E. None of the above

13. If Earl can type 80 words in three minutes, how long will it take him to type 400 words, working at the same rate?
    A. 15 minutes
    B. 16 minutes
    C. 18 minutes
    D. 20 minutes
    E. 22 minutes

14. Robin earns $120 in five days. At the same rate of pay, how much will she earn in eight days?
    A. $180
    B. $192
    C. $200
    D. $240
    E. $248

15. If Jason can read $\frac{3}{8}$ of a book in 6 days, how many days will it take him to read the entire book, at the same rate?
    A. 10 days
    B. 12 days
    C. 14 days
    D. 16 days
    E. None of the above

16. On a map, 6" represents 240 miles. How many miles would 9" represent?
    A. 300 miles
    B. 320 miles
    C. 360 miles
    D. 400 miles
    E. 420 miles

Practice Test

1. What is the average of all the multiples of 5 from 5 to 50, inclusive?
   - A. 5
   - B. 11
   - C. 21
   - D. 26.5
   - E. 27.5

2. A race car driver averages 159 miles per hour for 19 laps driven. How fast must he go in his 20th lap to attain an average of 160 miles per hour?
   - A. 160
   - B. 161
   - C. 175
   - D. 179
   - E. 180

3. In a standard deck of cards, there are 13 cards with hearts, 13 with spades, 13 with diamonds, and 13 with clubs. If one card is chosen from the deck at random, what is the probability that it will be a heart or a diamond?
   - A. $\frac{1}{4}$
   - B. $\frac{1}{2}$
   - C. $\frac{1}{13}$
   - D. $\frac{2}{13}$
   - E. $\frac{13}{39}$

4. A cookie jar contains 12 chocolate chip, 6 vanilla, 5 raisin, and 2 oatmeal cookies. What is the probability of randomly picking a raisin cookie on the first draw?
   - A. $\frac{1}{3}$
   - B. $\frac{1}{4}$
   - C. $\frac{1}{5}$
   - D. $\frac{1}{6}$
   - E. None of the above

5. Jeff bought a radio for $14.99, earphones for $9.99, and a cassette tape for $7.99. Including a sales tax of 6%, what was the total bill?
   - A. $30.99
   - B. $34.95
   - C. $33.95
   - D. $32.99
   - E. $35.00

6. Eric bought a suitcase for $39.95, a garment bag for $79.95, and a briefcase for $24.99. If the sales tax on these items is 6%, how much will the sales tax be?
   - A. $ 7.24
   - B. $ 8.69
   - C. $ 9.89
   - D. $ 10.14
   - E. None of the above

7. The price of a gallon of Number 2 fuel oil went from $0.64 to $0.68 per gallon. What was the percent of increase in the price of a gallon?
   - A. $\frac{1}{16}\%$
   - B. 4%
   - C. $5\frac{15}{17}\%$
   - D. $6\frac{1}{4}\%$
   - E. None of the above

8. Last year, Tom earned $160 shoveling snow. This year, he earned $120. Compared to his earnings last year, by what percentage did his earnings decrease?
   - A. 20%
   - B. 25%
   - C. 30%
   - D. 33%
   - E. 40%

9. Betsy's softball team won 47 games, lost 15 games, and tied none. What fractional part of the games played did the team win?

A. $\dfrac{47}{15}$ B. $\dfrac{15}{47}$

C. $\dfrac{32}{47}$ D. $\dfrac{15}{62}$

E. $\dfrac{47}{62}$

10. Adam watches television for 3 hours each weekday and a total of 12 hours on the weekend. What fraction represents the amount of time he spends watching TV each week?

A. $\dfrac{15}{24}$ B. $\dfrac{27}{148}$

C. $\dfrac{9}{56}$ D. $\dfrac{29}{168}$

E. $\dfrac{33}{168}$

11. Matt saves 20% on a $110 bowling ball but must pay 6% sales tax. What is the total amount that he must pay?

A. $ 88.00
B. $ 93.28
C. $ 96.00
D. $140.80
E. None of the above

12. In a metropolitan area, the assessed value of a house is determined as 60% of the house's market value, and the property tax is 3.9% of the assessed value. What is the property tax on a house with a market value of $105,000?

A. $1,596
B. $1,638
C. $2,457
D. $3,990
E. None of the above

13. In the 9th grade, 7 of every 10 students is a girl. If there are 200 students in the 9th grade, how many of the students are girls?

A. 120
B. 130
C. 140
D. 150
E. 160

14. In a factory, 15 of every 300 light bulbs tested were defective. At the same rate, if 1,200 bulbs are tested, how many of them would be defective?

A. 40
B. 50
C. 60
D. 80
E. 90

15. If $\dfrac{3}{5}$ of a job can be completed in 6 weeks, how long will it take to complete the entire job, working at the same rate?

A. 10 weeks
B. 12 weeks
C. 15 weeks
D. 20 weeks
E. 22 weeks

16. On a map, 2 inches represents 200 miles. How many miles would 7 inches represent?

A. 400 miles
B. 600 miles
C. 700 miles
D. 1,400 miles
E. None of the above

SKILL BUILDER THREE

Exponents

An exponent tells you how many times to write the base in a multiplication problem. For example, 3^2 is read as "three to the second power" or "three squared." The 3 is called the **base**. The 2 is called the **power** or **exponent**. When finding powers involving fractions and decimals, pay special attention to the fraction and decimal rules.

Example	Solution
$(.03)^2$	$.03^2$ means $.03 \times .03 = .0009$

Example	Solution
$\left(\dfrac{2}{3}\right)^2$	$\left(\dfrac{2}{3}\right)^2$ means $\dfrac{2}{3} \times \dfrac{2}{3} = \dfrac{4}{9}$

One raised to any power is 1.

Example	Solution
1^4	$1^4 = 1 \times 1 \times 1 \times 1 = 1$

Any number raised to the first power is that number.

Example	Solution
8^1	$8^1 = 8$

Any number (except zero) raised to the zero power is 1. This is a special case.

Example	Solution
9^0	$9^0 = 1$

Number Concepts

Commutative Law

Adding $6 + 4$ or $4 + 6$ yields an answer of 10. There is no change in the answer when adding any two integers. This is an example of the **commutative law** of addition. Similarly, $3 \times 5 = 5 \times 3$ illustrates the commutative law for multiplication.

Associative Law

To add more than two integers, such as $8 + 7 + 5$, add them together as $(8 + 7) + 5$, which is $15 + 5 = 20$. You can also add them as $8 + (7 + 5)$ which is $8 + 12 = 20$. In either case, the sum is the same. This is an illustration of the **associative law** of addition. Similarly, $2 \times (3 \times 4) = (2 \times 3) \times 4$ illustrates the associative law for multiplication.

Distributive Law

Multiplying the sum of two numbers, $4 + 2$, by another number, 6, is an example of the **distributive law** of multiplication over addition: $6(4 + 2)$. The value of this expression is $6(6) = 36$ but the answer can also be found in the following way:

$$6(4 + 2) = 6(4) + 6(2)$$
$$= 24 + 12$$
$$= 36$$

The integer 6 is said to be distributed over the sum of 4 and 2.

Even and Odd Numbers

A number that is divisible by 2 is an even number.

$$414, \quad 3{,}050, \quad 8{,}886$$

A number that is not even is an odd number.

$$1, \quad 357, \quad 5{,}129$$

Zero is an even integer.

Sums and Differences of Even and Odd Numbers

The sum of two even numbers or two odd numbers is always an even number.

$$6 + 4 = 10 \qquad 13 + 15 = 28$$

The sum of an even number and an odd number is always an odd number.

$$8 + 7 = 15 \qquad 16 + 21 = 37$$

The difference between two even numbers or two odd numbers is always an even number.

$$12 - 8 = 4 \qquad 15 - 7 = 8$$

The difference between an even number and an odd number is always an odd number.

$$8 - 5 = 3 \qquad 25 - 18 = 7$$

Products of Even and Odd Numbers

The product of two even numbers is always an even number.

$$4 \times 8 = 32$$

The product of two odd numbers is always an odd number.

$$3 \times 7 = 21$$

The product of an even number and an odd number is always an even number.

$$8 \times 9 = 72 \qquad 7 \times 12 = 84$$

Factors, Primes, and Factorials

Factors

When two or more whole numbers are multiplied, each is a factor of the product. The numbers 1, 2, 4, and 8 are factors of 8 because the product of both 1 and 8 and 2 and 4 is 8.

$$1 \times 8 = 8$$
$$2 \times 4 = 8$$

The positive factors of 8 are {1, 2, 4, 8}. If you divide 8 by each of the factors, the remainder is 0.

Example

What is the set of positive factors of each of the following numbers?

10   **Solution**   {1, 2, 5, 10}
34   **Solution**   {1, 2, 17, 34}
20   **Solution**   {1, 2, 4, 5, 10, 20}
48   **Solution**   {1, 2, 3, 4, 6, 8, 12, 16, 24, 48}

In arithmetic, a multiple of a number is a number that is the *product* of the given number and another *factor*. For example, the numbers 2 and 4 both have the number 2 as a factor. Therefore, 2 and 4 are multiples of 2. Also {6, 12, 18, 24, ...} represents the positive multiples of 6.

Some numbers have exactly two different positive factors: the number itself and 1. These numbers, such as 2, 3, 5, and 7, are called **prime numbers**. Numbers that have more than 2 different positive factors are called **composite numbers**. Examples of these numbers are 6, 8, 9, and 15. The number 1 is neither prime nor composite since it has only 1 positive factor. (1 and -1 are called **units**.)

Example

What are all the prime numbers from 1 to 40?

Solution

{2, 3, 5, 7, 11, 13, 17, 19, 23, 29, 31, 37}

If the factorization of a number contains only prime numbers it is called a **prime factorization** of that number. A prime factorization of 8 is 2 • 2 • 2, of 24 is 2 • 2 • 2 • 3, of 35 is 5 • 7.

Example

What is a prime factorization of 40?

Solution

How do you find the prime factorization of a composite number such as 40? Begin by finding any two factors of 40, say 8 and 5. Then express each factor as a product of two other factors.

$$40 = 5 \bullet 8$$
$$5 \bullet 2 \bullet 4$$
$$5 \bullet 2 \bullet 2 \bullet 2$$

or $2^3 \bullet 5$ in exponential form

Example

Which of the following statement(s) is (are) true?

  I.   51 is not a prime number.
  II.   All composite numbers are even.
  III.   The product of two primes is always composite.

(A) I only   (D) I and III
(B) III only   (E) II and III
(C) I and II

Solution

Examine statement I. Attempt to prove the other statements false by supplying at least one counter example. Test different numbers in each statement.

I is true. 51 is not a prime number.
II is false, since 15 (3 × 5) is odd.
III is true, since any number that is a product of two primes will always have those two primes as factors. The answer is D.

Factorials

For a positive integer n, the product of all the positive integers less than or equal to n is called a factorial. Factorial n is written $n!$

For example $1! = 1$
$\quad\quad\quad 2! = 2 \bullet 1 = 2$
$\quad\quad\quad 3! = 3 \bullet 2 \bullet 1 = 6$
$\quad\quad\quad 4! = 4 \bullet 3 \bullet 2 \bullet 1 = 24$
$\quad\quad\quad 5! = 5 \bullet 4 \bullet 3 \bullet 2 \bullet 1 = 120$, and $0!$ is defined as 1 (to make some mathematical formulas behave nicely)

Absolute Value, Square Roots, and Irrational Numbers

The absolute value of an integer is the distance the number is from zero on the number line.

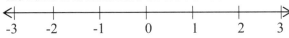

Thus, the absolute value of 3 or of -3 is 3, since each number is 3 units from 0. This is written as $|3| = 3$ and read as "the absolute value of 3 equals 3." Similarly, $|-3| = 3$ is read as "the absolute value of -3 is 3."

Example
What is the value of $|-16| - |3|$?

Solution
$|-16| = 16 \quad\quad |3| = 3$
$|-16| - |3| = 16 - 3 = 13$

Example
Evaluate $|-4| + |8|$.

Solution
$|-4| = 4 \quad\quad |8| = 8$
$|-4| + |8| = 4 + 8 = 12$

Roots of Numbers
You know that $9 = 3^2$. Since 9 is 3 squared, it is said that the square root of 9 is 3. It is written as $\sqrt{9} = 3$. The **principal square root** (or positive square root) of 9 is 3. What is the positive square root of 25? Since $5^2 = 25$, then $\sqrt{25} = 5$.

Example
Simplify the following:
$\sqrt{49} = 7$
$\sqrt{100} = 10$
$-\sqrt{4} = -2$

Example
Simplify the following:
$\sqrt{25} + \sqrt{4} = 5 + 2 = 7$
$\sqrt{36} - \sqrt{16} = 6 - 4 = 2$
$\left(\sqrt{25}\right)\left(\sqrt{36}\right) = 5 \bullet 6 = 30$

The square roots of numbers that are not perfect squares neither terminate nor repeat. For example, $\sqrt{5}$ is approximately equal to 2.2361 and belongs to the set of irrational numbers. Likewise, $\sqrt{2}$, $-\sqrt{3}$, $\sqrt{11}$, and $\sqrt[3]{5}$ are also irrational numbers.

Example
Simplify each expression by removing factors that form perfect squares.
$\sqrt{15}$
Since 15 does not contain a perfect square (other than 1) among its factors, it is said to be in simplified form.
$\sqrt{20}$
The factors of 20 are 1, 2, 4, 5, 10, and 20. Since 4 is a perfect square we can use $(4)(5) = 20$ as follows:
$\sqrt{20} = \sqrt{(4)(5)} = \left(\sqrt{4}\right)\left(\sqrt{5}\right) = 2\sqrt{5}$.
$\dfrac{\sqrt{40}}{2}$
The factors of 40 are 1, 2, 4, 5, 8, 10, 20, and 40. Since 4 is a perfect square we can use $(4)(10) = 40$ as follows:
$\dfrac{\sqrt{40}}{2} = \dfrac{\sqrt{(4)(10)}}{2} = \dfrac{\left(\sqrt{4}\right)\left(\sqrt{10}\right)}{2} = \dfrac{2\sqrt{10}}{2} = \sqrt{10}$
$2\sqrt{72}$
The factors of 72 are 1, 2, 3, 4, 6, 8, 9, 12, 18, 24, 36, and 72. The perfect squares are 1, 4, 9, and 36. To simplify, use the largest perfect square, which is 36:
$2\sqrt{72} = 2\sqrt{(36)(2)} = 2\left(\sqrt{36}\right)\left(\sqrt{2}\right) = 2(6)\sqrt{2} = 12\sqrt{2}$

Orientation Exercises

1. $4^3 - 3^2 + 8^0 = ?$

   A. 11
   B. 14
   C. 47
   D. 53
   E. 56

2. What is the sum of all the ODD integers from 11 to 21, inclusive?

   A. 64
   B. 80
   C. 85
   D. 96
   E. 100

3. Which of the following can be expressed as the product of two consecutive ODD integers?

   A. 9
   B. 21
   C. 27
   D. 63
   E. 77

4. What are the positive factors of 64?

   A. {1, 64}
   B. {1, 2, 32, 64}
   C. {1, 2, 4, 8, 16, 32, 64}
   D. {1, 2, 4, 6, 8, 12, 16, 32, 64}
   E. All of the above

5. What is the prime factorization of 72?

   A. $1 \bullet 72$
   B. $2 \bullet 4 \bullet 9$
   C. $2 \bullet 3^3 \bullet 4$
   D. $2 \bullet 3^2 \bullet 3$
   E. $2^3 \bullet 3^2$

6. Evaluate 6!

   A. 0
   B. 1
   C. 6
   D. 36
   E. 720

7. How many prime numbers are there between 20 and 30?

   A. 1
   B. 2
   C. 3
   D. 4
   E. 5

8. Which one of the following is an irrational number?

   A. 3.14
   B. $|-3 + 2|$
   C. 0
   D. $\sqrt{121}$
   E. $\sqrt{10}$

Practice Exercises

1. What is the value of $(.02)^2$?

   A. .4   D. .0004
   B. .04   E. .22
   C. .004

2. $4^3 \cdot 3^2 \cdot 2^3 = ?$

   A.   576   D. 3,072
   B. 1,152   E. 4,608
   C. 2,304

3. Which of the following numbers can be evenly divided by both 4 and 9?

   A. 1,350   D. 5,756
   B. 2,268   E. None of the above
   C. 4,700

4. Which of the following numbers are divisible by 3?

   (I)   242
   (II)   45,027
   (III)   804,597

   A. II only   D. II and III
   B. III only   E. I, II, and III
   C. I and II

5. $\dfrac{3^{14}}{27^4} = ?$

   A. $\dfrac{1}{9}$ D. 9

   B. 1   E. 27
   C. 3

6. What are the positive factors of 16?
   A. $\{1, 16\}$
   B. $\{1, 2, 8, 16\}$
   C. $\{1, 4, 8, 16\}$
   D. $\{1, 2, 4, 8, 16\}$
   E. $\{1, 2, 4, 6, 8, 16\}$

7. What is the prime factorization of 144?
   A. $1 \cdot 144$
   B. $2 \cdot 2 \cdot 36$
   C. $2 \cdot 2 \cdot 4 \cdot 9$
   D. $2^4 \cdot 3^2$
   E. $2^2 \cdot 3^4$

8. Evaluate $\dfrac{6!}{3!5!}$

   A. 0   D. 90
   B. 1   E. 720
   C. 48

9. What is the prime factorization of 210?

   A. $2 \cdot 5 \cdot 21$
   B. $3 \cdot 7 \cdot 11$
   C. $2 \cdot 3 \cdot 5 \cdot 7$
   D. $2 \cdot 3 \cdot 7 \cdot 11$
   E. $2 \cdot 105$

10. What is the value of $|\text{-}20| - |\text{-}5|$?

    A. -25   D. 25
    B. -15   E. 100
    C. 15

11. $\sqrt{32} = ?$

    A. $2\sqrt{8}$ D. $3\sqrt{4}$
    B. $2\sqrt{4}$ E. 6
    C. $4\sqrt{2}$

Practice Test

1. $8^1 - 5^0 + 3^2 = ?$

    A. 9   D. 14
    B. 12   E. 16
    C. 13

2. The numerical value of $11^0 + 11^1 + 11^2 =$

    A. 33   D. 132
    B. 122   E. None of the
    C. 123   above

3. $2 \times 346 + 3 \times 346 + 5 \times 346 = ?$
    A. 1,730
    B. 3,460
    C. 5,190
    D. 10,380
    E. None of the above

4. If $\dfrac{5}{n}$ is an even number, which of the following could be a value of n?

    A. $\dfrac{1}{5}$ D. $\dfrac{5}{3}$

    B. $\dfrac{2}{5}$ E. $\dfrac{6}{5}$

    C. $\dfrac{5}{6}$

5. If $4 \bullet 3^x$ is divisible by just 9 positive integers, then $x = ?$

    A. 1   D. 4
    B. 2   E. 5
    C. 3

6. Which set of numbers contains only primes?

    A. {1, 2, 3, 5}
    B. {17, 13, 5, 0}
    C. {0, 1, 33, 51}
    D. {9, 7, 5, 3}
    E. {2, 7, 13, 19}

7. In the figure, arcs are drawn above the number line every 3 units and below the number line every 2 units. If the arcs meet at P and Q, at which of the following points on the number line will the arcs also meet?

    A. 252   D. 255
    B. 253   E. 256
    C. 254

8. Evaluate $(3n)!$ for $n = 2$.

    A. 6   D. 120
    B. 12   E. 720
    C. 36

9. $\sqrt{72} = ?$

    A. $2\sqrt{18}$ D. $4\sqrt{18}$
    B. $2\sqrt{6}$ E. $6\sqrt{2}$
    C. $3\sqrt{8}$

10. $\sqrt{63}$ divided by which of the following numbers yields a rational number?

    A. $\sqrt{21}$ D. $\sqrt{7}$
    B. $\sqrt{3}$ E. $\sqrt{2}$
    C. $\sqrt{9}$

ELEMENTARY ALGEBRA
SKILL BUILDER FOUR

Multiplication of Signed Numbers

Rules for Multiplying Two Signed Numbers
1. If the signs of the numbers are alike, the product is positive.
2. If the signs of the numbers are different, the product is negative.

Example
What is the product of (-6) and (-5)?

Solution
The signs are alike, the answer is positive.
$$(-6)(-5) = +30$$

Example
Find $(15)\left(-\dfrac{1}{5}\right)$.

Solution
The signs are different, the answer is negative.
$$\left(\frac{\overset{3}{15}}{1}\right)\left(-\frac{1}{\underset{1}{5}}\right) = -\frac{3}{1} = \text{-3}$$

Rules for Multiplying More Than Two Signed Numbers
1. If the problem contains an even number of minus signs, the product is positive.
2. If the problem contains an odd number of minus signs, the product is negative.

Example
$(4)(-3)(8)(-2) = +192$
The problem has two minus signs; since 2 is an even number, the product is positive.

Example
$(-2)(-3)(4)(-5) = -120$
The problem has three minus signs; since 3 is an odd number, the product is negative.

Evaluation of Algebraic Expressions

Example
Evaluate $5a + 3 - 3b + 7$ if $a = 4$ and $b = 5$.

Solution
Substitute the given number values for their respective letters:
$$5a + 3 - 3b + 7$$
$$5(4) + 3 - 3(5) + 7$$
Perform the required operations, remembering to multiply before adding or subtracting:
$$20 + 3 - 15 + 7 = 15$$

Example
Evaluate $x^2 - y^2$ if $x = 5$ and $y = 4$.

Solution
(Substitute)	$5^2 - 4^2$
(Powers first)	$25 - 16$
(Subtract)	9

Writing Algebraic Expressions and Equations

In order to solve problems algebraically, it is necessary to express number relations by the use of symbols. English statements must be translated into mathematical symbols.

In the following examples, pay close attention to the underlined words that suggest which mathematical symbols to use. The letter "*n*" is used for the word "number" in these examples. Any letter can be used.

a. A number <u>increased by</u> 5
    "increased by" indicates addition $n + 5$
b. Seven <u>less than</u> a number
    "less than" indicates subtraction $n - 7$
c. Seven <u>decreased by</u> a number
    "decreased by" indicates subtraction;
    in this case the number is being
    subtracted from 7 $7 - n$
d. The <u>product</u> of 3 and a number
    "product" indicates multiplication $3n$

e. The <u>sum</u> of a number and one-fourth of the number

"sum" indicates addition,

"of" indicates multiplication

$$n + \frac{1}{4}n$$

f. A number <u>divided</u> by 6

Division is usually written as a fraction

$$\frac{n}{6}$$

g. Five more than twice a number

"more than" indicates addition

$$5 + 2n \text{ or } 2n + 5$$

h. Half of a number decreased by 3

(only one order is correct)

$$\frac{1}{2}n - 3$$

When writing equations from written statements, the verb suggests where to put the equal sign.

i. Ten more than 4 times a number <u>is</u> 46.

Replace the verb "is" with an equal sign.

$$4n + 10 = 46$$

j. Six times a number <u>equals</u> 21 more than 3 times the number.

The verb "equals" tells us where to put the = sign.

$$6n = 21 + 3n$$

Simplifying Algebraic Fractions

A fraction is in its simplest form when the numerator and denominator have no common integral factor except 1 or -1.

Example

Simplify $\dfrac{16xy}{24x^2}$.

Solution

Find the GCD (greatest common divisor) and reduce the fraction to its lowest terms. Here the GCD is $8x$.

$$\frac{16xy}{24x^2} = \frac{\overset{2}{16}\ x\overset{1}{y}}{\underset{3}{24}\ \underset{x}{x^2}} = \frac{2y}{3x}$$

When fractions contain polynomials, one method is to factor first and then reduce to lowest terms.

Example

Simplify $\dfrac{x^2 + 4x - 12}{5x - 10}$.

Solution

First factor, and then reduce:

$$\frac{x^2 + 4x - 12}{5x - 10} = \frac{(x+6)\overset{1}{\cancel{(x-2)}}}{5\underset{1}{\cancel{(x-2)}}} = \frac{x+6}{5}$$

Example

Simplify $\dfrac{4-a}{a^2 - 16}$.

Solution

Factor the numerator, showing -1 as one of the factors:

$$\frac{4-a}{a^2-16} = \frac{-1\overset{1}{\cancel{(a-4)}}}{(a+4)\underset{1}{\cancel{(a-4)}}} = \frac{-1}{a+4}$$

Orientation Exercises

1. What is the product of (-7) and (+8)?

   A. -56 D. 1

   B. $-1\frac{1}{7}$ E. 56

   C. -1

2. What is $(-8)\left(-\frac{3}{7}\right)(-7)$?

   A. -24

   B. $-2\frac{4}{7}$

   C. 24

   D. $55\frac{4}{7}$

   E. None of the above

3. If $a = 4$ and $b = 6$, what is $\frac{3a+b}{2}$?

   A. 3 D. 11

   B. $6\frac{1}{2}$ E. 15

   C. 9

4. If $c = 7$ and $d = 8$, what is $c^2 - 2d$?

   A. -2 D. 48

   B. 6 E. 65

   C. 33

5. If $c = 3$ and $d = 7$, what is $20 - 2c + 4d$?

   A. 14 D. 42

   B. 18 E. 54

   C. 22

   | Translate the following expressions to mathematical statements or equations, using the letter n to represent the variable. |
   ---

6. Four times a number n decreased by 7 = ?

   A. $4n + 7$ D. $4n - 7$

   B. $7 - 4n$ E. $4 - 7n$

   C. $4 + 7n$

7. Twice a number n increased by 3 is 15.

   A. $2n - 3 = 15$
   B. $2n + 3 = 15$
   C. $6n = 15$
   D. $3n + 2 = 15$
   E. $3n - 2 = 15$

8. $\frac{6xy}{18y^3} = ?$

   A. $\frac{2xy}{6y^2}$ D. $\frac{xy}{3y^2}$

   B. $3xy^2$ E. $\frac{2x}{3y^2}$

   C. $\frac{x}{3y^2}$

9. Simplify $\frac{2-a}{a^2-10a+16}$, $a \ne 2, a \ne 8$.

   A. $a + 8$

   B. $\frac{a-8}{-1}$

   C. $\frac{1}{a+8}$

   D. $\frac{-1}{a-8}$

   E. $11a + 8$

10. Simplify $\frac{3x^2-10x-8}{x-4}$, $x \ne 4$.

    A. $x - 4$
    B. $x - 2$
    C. $3x - 4$
    D. $3x - 2$
    E. $3x + 2$

Practice Exercises

1. What is the product of $\left(-\dfrac{3}{5}\right)$ and (-15)?

   A. -25 D. $15\dfrac{3}{5}$

   B. -9 E. 25

   C. 9

2. What is the product of (-7), $(+5)$, and (-1)?

   A. -40 D. 13

   B. -35 E. 35

   C. -3

3. What is $\left(-\dfrac{1}{3}\right) \div \left(\dfrac{5}{9}\right)$?

   A. $-\dfrac{3}{5}$ D. $-1\dfrac{2}{3}$

   B. $-\dfrac{5}{18}$ E. $-5\dfrac{2}{7}$

   C. $-\dfrac{2}{9}$

4. Which of the following must be positive?

   I. The sum of two negative numbers.
   II. The product of two negative numbers.
   III. The product of three negative numbers.

   A. I only   D. I and II only
   B. II only   E. II and III only
   C. III only

5. If $a = 5$ and $b = 4$, evaluate $10b - 5a$.
   A. 5 D. 30
   B. 15 E. 70
   C. 25

6. If $e = 8$ and $f = 3$, evaluate $e^2 - f^3$.
   A. 7 D. 49
   B. 37 E. 91
   C. 47

7. If $m = 12$ and $n = 4$, evaluate $\dfrac{2m+8}{n}$.
   A. 1 D. 16
   B. 4 E. 24
   C. 8

8. What is the value of xy^2z^3 if $x = 2$, $y = -2$, and $z = 3$?
   A. -216 D. 96
   B. -72 E. 216
   C. 72

9. "Five times a number n decreased by 10" can be written as:
   A. $5 - 10n$ D. $10n - 5$
   B. $10 - 5n$ E. $50n$
   C. $5n - 10$

10. "Five less than 3 times a number n" can be expressed as:
    A. $3n + 5$ D. $3n - 5$
    B. $5 - 3n$ E. $15n$
    C. $5 + 3n$

11. "The sum of 8 and a number n all divided by 5" is

    A. $8 + \dfrac{n}{5}$ D. $\dfrac{8n}{5}$

    B. $\dfrac{8}{n} + 5$ E. $\dfrac{8+n}{5}$

    C. $8n + 5$

12. "When 4 times a number n is increased by 5, the result is the same as when 100 is decreased by the number n" can be written as:
    A. $4n - 5 = n + 100$ D. $4n + 5 = 100 - n$
    B. $5n + 4 = 100 - n$ E. $5 + 4n = n - 100$
    C. $5n - 4 = n - 100$

13. Simplify $\dfrac{4r+20}{r+5}$, $r \neq -5$.

    A. $\dfrac{1}{4}$ D. 8

    B. 4 E. $4r + 4$

    C. $3r + 4$

14. Simplify $\dfrac{24b+8}{5b+(1-2b)}$, $b \neq -\dfrac{1}{3}$.

    A. $\dfrac{16}{1-2b}$ D. $\dfrac{8b}{b+1}$

    B. 8 E. None of the above

    C. 24

Practice Test

1. Find $(-4)\left(-\dfrac{1}{4}\right)(5)\left(-\dfrac{1}{5}\right)$.

    A. $-\dfrac{2}{9}$ D. $1\dfrac{9}{20}$

    B. -1 E. $9\dfrac{9}{20}$

    C. 1

2. What is $(-1)(-9)(+5)(-11)$?

    A. 495   D. -25
    B. 16   E. -495
    C. -16

3. $\left(-4\dfrac{1}{2}\right)\left(\dfrac{5}{9}\right)\left(-2\dfrac{2}{3}\right) = \,?$

    A. $-6\dfrac{11}{18}$

    B. $6\dfrac{2}{3}$

    C. $7\dfrac{13}{18}$

    D. $8\dfrac{5}{27}$

    E. None of the above

4. Which of the following must be negative?

    I. The sum of two negative numbers.
    II. The product of two negative numbers.
    III. The quotient of two negative numbers.

    A. I only
    B. I and II only
    C. II and III only
    D. I and III only
    E. I, II and III

5. If $x = 8$ and $y = 5$, evaluate $\dfrac{3x}{9-y}$.

    A. 1
    B. 4
    C. 6
    D. 7
    E. None of the above

6. If $a = 5$ and $b = 3$, evaluate $a^2 + b^3$.

    A. 16   D. 37
    B. 19   E. 52
    C. 34

7. If $a = 5$ and $b = 3$, evaluate $48 - 6a + b^2$.

    A. 9   D. 27
    B. 18   E. 48
    C. 24

8. If $a = -3$, $b = 4$, and $c = -5$, then the product abc is how much greater than the sum $a + b + c$?

    A. -64 D. 56
    B. -56 E. 64
    C. 48

9. The statement "a number n increased by twice another number b is equal to 18" can be written as:

    A. $2nb = 18$ D. $2n + 2b = 18$
    B. $n + 2b = 18$ E. $2n + b = 18$
    C. $n + 2n = 18$

10. "The product of 3 and a number n decreased by 15" can be written as:

    A. $3n - 15$ D. $15n - 3$
    B. $15 - 3n$ E. $45n$
    C. $3 - 15n$

11. "The sum of 4 and a number n all divided by 5" can be expressed as:

A. $4 + \dfrac{n}{5}$

B. $\dfrac{4}{5} + n$

C. $\dfrac{4+n}{5}$

D. $\dfrac{4n}{5}$

E. None of the above

12. "A number n equals 7 more than half the number" can be written as:

A. $n + 7 = \dfrac{1}{2}n$

B. $n + 7n = \dfrac{1}{2}$

C. $n = 7n + \dfrac{1}{2}$

D. $n = 3\dfrac{1}{2} + n$

E. $n = 7 + \dfrac{1}{2}n$

13. Simplify $\dfrac{m^2 - x^2}{m^2 + mx}$, $m \neq -x$.

A. x

B. $\dfrac{m-x}{m}$

C. $-x$

D. $-\dfrac{x}{m}$

E. $\dfrac{m+x}{m}$

14. Simplify $\dfrac{a^2 + 1}{a + 1}$, $a \neq -1$

A. $a + 1$

B. $a - 1$

C. a

D. $\dfrac{1}{a}$

E. None of the above

Evaluating a Formula

A formula is an instruction written in the symbols of algebra. To use any formula, simply replace a value that is given in the problem for the appropriate letter. The order of operations rule must be followed.

Example

Changing Fahrenheit temperature to centigrade temperature is done by using the formula $C = \frac{5}{9}(F - 32)$. Find the centigrade temperature that corresponds to 41° Fahrenheit.

Solution

(Substitute 41 for F) $\qquad C = \frac{5}{9}(41 - 32)$

(Simplify the parentheses) $\qquad C = \frac{5}{9}(9)$

(Multiply) $\qquad C = \frac{5}{\overset{}{9}} \cdot \frac{\overset{1}{9}}{1} = \frac{5}{1}$

$\qquad C = 5°$ centigrade

Example

$R = \frac{1}{2}wt^2$. What is the value of R when $w = 16$ and $t = 3$?

Solution

(Substitute) $\qquad R = \frac{1}{2}(16)(3)^2$

(Find the power) $\qquad R = \frac{1}{2}(16)(9)$

(Multiply) $\qquad R = \frac{1}{\underset{1}{2}} \cdot \frac{\overset{8}{16}}{1} \cdot \frac{9}{1} = \frac{72}{1} = 72$

Equations Containing Fractions

If an equation contains one or more fractions or decimals, clear it by multiplying each term by the LCD (lowest common denominator).

Example

Solve for x: $\dfrac{5x - 7}{3} = x - 5$

Solution

Multiply each side by 3.

$$^1\cancel{3}\left(\frac{5x - 7}{\cancel{3}_1}\right) = 3(x - 5)$$

(To isolate the variable $\qquad 5x - 7 = 3x - 15$
subtract $3x$ from both sides) $\qquad 2x - 7 = -15$
(Add 7) $\qquad 2x = -8$
(Divide by 2) $\qquad x = -4$

Factoring Quadratic Equations

To solve a quadratic equation:
- Write the equation in standard form (set it equal to zero).
- Factor 1 side of the equation.
- Set *each* factor equal to zero.
- Solve each equation.

Example

What is the smaller solution to the equation $3x^2 + 7x - 6 = 0$?

Solution

The equation is already in standard form. The simplest way to solve this problem is to find the 2 solutions and then choose the smaller one. The solutions can be found by factoring

$$3x^2 + 7x - 6 = 0$$
$$(3x - 2)(x + 3) = 0$$

Set each factor equal to zero

$$3x - 2 = 0 \qquad\qquad x + 3 = 0$$
$$3x = 2 \qquad\qquad\qquad x = -3$$
$$x = \frac{2}{3}$$

$x = -3$ is the smaller of the 2 solutions.

Miscellaneous Word Problems

Solving word problems

Step 1. Read the problem carefully.
Step 2. Select a suitable replacement for the unknown amount(s).
Step 3. Set up an equation using the information in the problem.
Step 4. Solve the equation.
Step 5. Answer the question in the problem.
Step 6. Check your result.

Example

The sum of three consecutive integers is 57. Find the numbers.

Solution

Step 1. Read carefully.
Step 2. Let x = first consecutive integer
$x + 1$ = second consecutive integer
$x + 2$ = third consecutive integer
Step 3. $x + (x + 1) + (x + 2) = 57$
$$3x + 3 = 57$$
$$3x = 54$$
Step 4. $x = 18$
Step 5. If $x = 18$, then $x + 1 = 19$, and $x + 2 = 20$.
Therefore, the 3 consecutive integers are 18, 19, and 20.
Step 6. 18, 19, and 20 are consecutive integers, and $18 + 19 + 20 = 57$.

Orientation Exercises

1. The formula $A = \dfrac{x+y+z}{3}$ is used to find the average (A) of three numbers x, y, and z. What is the average of 86, 113, and 119?

   A. $102\dfrac{2}{3}$ D. 110

   B. 106   E. 160

   C. 108

2. In the formula $C = \dfrac{5}{9}(F-32)$, find C if $F = 68$.

   A. 1   D. 180

   B. 9   E. None of the above

   C. 20

3. Solve for x: $x + \dfrac{4}{3} = \dfrac{-20}{3}$

   A. -72   D. $\dfrac{16}{3}$

   B. $\dfrac{-46}{3}$ E. 8

   C. -8

4. Solve for s: $\dfrac{s}{4} - \dfrac{7}{2} = 4$

   A. 11   D. 30

   B. 14   E. None of the above

   C. 16

5. What is the larger solution to the equation $2x^2 + 9x - 5 = 0$?

   A. - 5   D. 2

   B. $-\dfrac{1}{2}$ E. 5

   C. $\dfrac{1}{2}$

6. Which of the following is a factorization of the polynomial $2x^2 + x - 6$?

   A. $2(x^2 + x - 3)$
   B. $(2x + 2)(x - 3)$
   C. $(2x + 3)(x - 2)$
   D. $(2x - 3)(x + 2)$
   E. $(2x + 6)(x - 1)$

7. David received three grades of 85, 92, and 100 on his first 3 tests. What must he get on the fourth test to get a 90 average?

   A. 83   D. 95

   B. 87   E. None of the above

   C. 90

8. Heidi must divide 870 bales of hay between three stables so that the second has 90 bales more than the first, but 150 less than the third. How many bales does the third stable receive?

   A. 180   D. 420

   B. 270   E. None of the above

   C. 310

Practice Exercises

1. Using the formula $P = 2(l + w)$, find P if $l = 40$ and $w = 20$.

   A. 60   D. 120
   B. 80   E. 140
   C. 100

2. In the formula $S = \dfrac{n}{2}(a + l)$, find S if $n = 5$, $a = 2$, and $l = 18$.

   A. 8   D. 25
   B. $12\dfrac{1}{2}$ E. 50
   C. $22\dfrac{1}{2}$

3. If $A = \dfrac{1}{2}h(b + c)$, find A if $h = 10$, $b = 8$, and $c = 12$.

   A. 25   D. 200
   B. 50   E. 400
   C. 100

4. The formula $c = 75 + 30(n - 5)$ is used to find the cost, c, of a taxi ride where n represents the number of $\dfrac{1}{5}$ miles of the ride. Find the cost of a taxi ride of $2\dfrac{2}{5}$ miles.

   A. \$2.10   D. \$7.35
   B. \$2.85   E. None of the above
   C. \$4.35

5. Solve for y: $\dfrac{y}{2} - \dfrac{y}{3} - 2 = 0$

   A. -2   D. $\dfrac{12}{5}$
   B. $\dfrac{5}{12}$ E. 12
   C. 2

6. Solve for x: $\dfrac{5x + 8}{x + 3} = 3$

   A. -2   D. $\dfrac{1}{8}$
   B. $-\dfrac{1}{2}$ E. 2
   C. $\dfrac{1}{2}$

7. Solve for n: $4 - \dfrac{3}{n} = \dfrac{5}{2}$

   A. $\dfrac{1}{2}$ D. 2
   B. $\dfrac{2}{3}$ E. None of the above
   C. $\dfrac{3}{4}$

8. Solve for a: $1 + \dfrac{1}{a} = \dfrac{2}{a} + 2$

   A. -8   D. 1
   B. -4   E. No solution
   C. -1

9. What is the smaller solution to the equation $x^2 - 2x = 0$?

   A. -2   D. 2
   B. 0   E. None of the above
   C. $\dfrac{1}{2}$

10. Which of the following is a factorization of the polynomial $x^2 - 7x - 18$?

    A. $(x - 18)(x + 1)$
    B. $(x + 9)(x - 2)$
    C. $(x - 9)(x - 2)$
    D. $(x - 9)(x + 2)$
    E. $(x - 6)(x - 3)$

11. Which of the following is a factorization of the expression $64 - 16a + a^2$?

    A. $(64 - a)(1 - a)$
    B. $(8 + a)(8 - a)$
    C. $(8 - a)(8 - a)$
    D. $(8 + a)(8 + a)$
    E. $(16 - a)(4 - a)$

12. Penny can knit 4 rows of a sweater in 5 minutes. How many *hours* will it take her to knit 300 rows?

    A.   4

    B. $6\frac{1}{4}$

    C. $12\frac{1}{2}$

    D.   240

    E.   375

13. The batting average of a baseball player is determined by the formula

$$B.A. = \frac{\text{number of hits}}{\text{number of at-bats}}$$

If a player with a .300 average gets 4 hits in his next 5 times at bat, what is his new average?

    A.   .467
    B.   .380
    C.   .304
    D.   .308
    E.   It cannot be determined.

14. Six times a number is 12 less than 10 times the number. What is the number?

    A.   3
    B.   6
    C.   12
    D.   18
    E.   24

Practice Test

1. If $C = \dfrac{5}{9}(F - 32)$, find C if $F = 32$.

   A. $\dfrac{5}{9}$ D. 5

   B. 0   E. 9

   C. 1

2. If $a = 3$ and $b = 4$, then find c if $c = \sqrt{a^2 + b^2}$.

   A. 5   D. 25

   B. 7   E. 49

   C. 15

3. If $s = 3$ and $t = 2$, then find w if $w = \dfrac{st^3}{(s+t)^2}$.

   A. $\dfrac{18}{25}$

   B. $\dfrac{24}{25}$

   C. $1\dfrac{4}{5}$

   D. $8\dfrac{16}{25}$

   E. None of the above

4. Using the formula $L = a + (n - 1)d$, find d if $L = 22$, $a = 7$, and $n = 6$.

   A. $1\dfrac{5}{6}$ D. 6

   B. 3   E. 75

   C. $5\dfrac{4}{5}$

5. Solve for w: $\dfrac{1}{2}w - \dfrac{1}{4} = \dfrac{3}{2}$

   A. 2   D. 4

   B. $2\dfrac{1}{2}$ E. 6

   C. $3\dfrac{1}{2}$

6. Solve for t: $\dfrac{5}{t+2} = \dfrac{4}{t-2}$

   A. -18   D. 9

   B. -2   E. 18

   C. 2

7. Solve for x: $\dfrac{5x}{6} = \dfrac{1}{12}$

   A. -10   D. 12

   B. $\dfrac{1}{10}$ E. No solution

   C. 10

8. Solve for e: $\dfrac{e+4}{e-2} = \dfrac{1}{3}$

   A. -7   D. $\dfrac{7}{2}$

   B. $-\dfrac{7}{2}$ E. 7

   C. $-\dfrac{5}{2}$

9. What is the larger solution to the equation $5x^2 + 9x - 2 = 0$?

   A. -2   D. 2

   B. $-\dfrac{1}{2}$ E. 5

   C. $\dfrac{1}{5}$

10. If the solutions of the equation
$2x^2 + kx - 8 = 0$ are $x = \dfrac{1}{2}$ and $x = -8$, then $k = ?$

   A.   -15   D.   8
   B.   -8   E.   15
   C.   -1

11. Which of the following is a factorization of the polynomial $2x^2 - 8x - 24$?

   A. $2(x^2 - 8x - 12)$
   B. $(2x - 4)(x + 6)$
   C. $(2x - 4)(x - 3)$
   D. $(2x + 4)(x - 6)$
   E. $(2x + 4)(x - 3)$

12. For all x, $(3x + 4)(x - 5) = ?$

   A. $3x^2 - 20$
   B. $3x^2 - 12x - 20$
   C. $3x^2 - 11x - 1$
   D. $3x^2 - 11x - 20$
   E. $3x^2 + 11x - 20$

13. A family drove 180 miles to Disneyland. If they left at 10:30 A.M. and got there at 3:00 P.M., what was their average speed in mph?

   A.   90   D. $32\dfrac{8}{11}$
   B.   45   E.   10
   C.   40

14. In an election with exactly 2 candidates, 373 votes were cast. If the winner's margin of victory was 87 votes, how many did she receive?

   A.   143
   B.   186
   C.   220
   D.   294
   E.   None of the above

15. Three times an angle's complement is 20° greater than its supplement. Find the angle measure.

   A.   35
   B.   45
   C.   55
   D.   65
   E.   155

Fundamental Operations with Monomials and Polynomials

Example

$(4x + 5y) + (2x - 11y) = ?$

Solution

Combine terms with the same variable:

$$4x + 5y + 2x - 11y$$
$$6x - 6y$$

Example

Simplify $(5a - 5b) - (3a - 7b)$.

Solution

The second polynomial is being subtracted. Change the signs of both terms in the second polynomial:

$$5a - 5b - 3a + 7b$$
$$2a + 2b$$

Example

Simplify $3a(4a^2 - 2a + 3)$.

Solution

Multiply ach term in the parentheses by $3a$:

$$3a(4a^2) + 3a(-2a) + 3a(3)$$
$$12a^3 - 6a^2 + 9a$$

Example

Multiply $(3x + 2)(x + 5)$.

Solution #1

$$3x + 2$$
$$x + 5$$
$$15x + 10$$
$$3x^2 + 2x$$
$$3x^2 + 17x + 10$$

Solution #2

$(3x + 2)(x + 5) = 3x^2$

$(3x + 2)(x + 5) = + 15x$

$(3x + 2)(x + 5) = + 2x$

$(3x + 2)(x + 5) = + 10$

$3x^2 + 17x + 10$

Factorization of Polynomials

Example

If $(x + a)(x + b) = x^2 + 7x + 12$ for all x, what is the value of $(a + b)$?

Solution

Factor $x^2 + 7x + 12$:

$$(x + 4)(x + 3)$$

Therefore $a = 4$ and $b = 3$, and the answer is the sum of $4 + 3$ or 7.

Example

The length of a rectangle is $x + 3$ inches and the width is $x - 2$ inches. What is the area, in terms of x, of the rectangle?

Solution

Length of rectangle $= x + 3$
Width of rectangle $= x - 2$
The area of the rectangle is found by multiplying the length by the width.

$$(x + 3)(x - 2) = x^2 + x - 6$$

Practice Exercises

1. A rectangle has a length of $x + 7$ and a width of $2x - 3$. If its perimeter is 32, what is the value of $3x$?

   A. 4   D. 36
   B. 12   E. 42
   C. 14

2. The height of a triangle is 5 less than double its base, which is $\frac{13}{2}$. Find the triangle's area.

   A. 13 inches   D. $11\frac{7}{2}$ inches
   B. 26 inches   E. $16\frac{1}{2}$ inches
   C. 52 inches

Practice Test

1. Maria has $(x + 14)$ pencils, Brian has $(x + 10)$ pencils, and Scott has $(x + 6)$ pencils. All these pencils are put into 3 empty boxes so that each box contains exactly y pencils. What is the value of y in terms of x?

   A. $10x$ D. $3x + 30$
   B. $x + 10$ E. $30x$
   C. $3x + 10$

2. If $6a - 4b = 9$, then $-12a + 8b = $?

   A. -18   D. 13
   B. -7   E. 18
   C. 11

3. The length of a rectangle is 5 more than twice its width. If the area of the rectangle is 42, what equation can be used for its width, x?

   A. $2x + 2(2x + 5) = 42$
   B. $x + (2x + 5) = 42$
   C. $x^2 + (2x + 5)^2 = 42$
   D. $2x^2 - 5x - 42 = 0$
   E. $2x^2 + 5x - 42 = 0$

4. If $(x + r)(x + s) = x^2 + 3x - 10$ for all x, then what is the value of $(r + s)$?

   A. -10   D. 7
   B. -3   E. 30
   C. 3

5. If a hexagon has three sides of length $x + 1$, two sides of length $x - 1$, and one side of length $2x$, what is its perimeter?

   A. $7x - 5$ D. $7x + 1$
   B. $7x - 1$ E. $7x + 5$
   C. $7x$

6. If $(x + w)(x + t) = x^2 + 3x - 4$ for all x, what is the value of $(w + t)$?

   A. -4   D. 3
   B. -3   E. 7
   C. -1

INTERMEDIATE ALGEBRA
SKILL BUILDER SEVEN

Linear Inequalities in One Variable

Solving an algebraic inequality is similar to solving an equation. The only difference is that in solving an inequality, you must remember to reverse the inequality symbol when you multiply or divide by a negative number.

Example

Solve for a: $\qquad\qquad a - 5 > 18$

Solution

Add 5 to both sides $\qquad\qquad a > 23$

Example

Solve for b: $\qquad\qquad 2b + 2 < -20$

Solution

Add -2 to both sides $\qquad\quad 2b < -22$
Divide by 2 $\qquad\qquad\qquad b < -11$

Example

Solve for x: $\qquad\qquad 7 - 4x > 27$

Solution

Add -7 to both sides $\qquad\quad -4x > 20$
Divide by -4 and reverse
the inequality sign $\qquad\qquad x < -5$

Remember: If $a < b$, then $a + c < b + c$.
$\qquad\qquad$ If $a < b$ and $c > 0$ (in other words c
$\qquad\qquad$ is positive) then $ac < bc$.
$\qquad\qquad$ If $a < b$ and $c < 0$ (c is negative)
$\qquad\qquad$ then $ac \geq bc$.

Absolute Value Equations and Inequalities

A combined sentence whose two parts are joined by the word *and* is called a **conjunction**. Its solution is the **intersection** of the solutions of its two component parts.

A combined sentence whose parts are joined by the word *or* is called a **disjunction**. Its solution is the **union** of its component parts.
In solving an equation or inequality involving **absolute value**, you should first rewrite the sentence as an equivalent conjunction or disjunction.

Example

Solve $|x + 4| = 2$.

Solution

$|x + 4| = 2$ is equivalent to a disjunction. It means $x + 4 = 2$ *or* $x + 4 = -2$.
Solve for x: $\qquad x = -2$ *or* $x = -6$

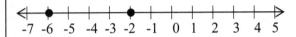

Example

Solve $|x + 4| > 2$.

Solution

$|x + 4| > 2$ is a disjunction. It means $x + 4 < -2$ *or* $x + 4 > 2$.
Solve for x: $\quad x < -6$ *or* $x > -2$

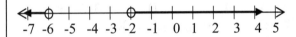

Example

Solve $|x + 4| < 2$.

Solution

$|x + 4| < 2$ is a conjunction. It means $x + 4 > -2$ *and* $x + 4 < 2$.
Solve for x: $\quad x > -6$ *and* $x < -2$

Another way of saying this is $x + 4$ is between -2 and 2.

$$-2 < x + 4 < 2$$
$$-6 < x < -2$$

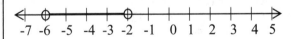

Operations with Integer Exponents

Rule 1. The exponent of the *product* of two powers of the same base is the sum of the exponents of the two powers.

$$a^m \bullet a^n = a^{m+n}$$
$$a^3 \bullet a^2 = a^{3+2} = a^5$$

Rule 2. The power of a *product* equals the product of the powers.

$$(ab)^m = a^m b^m$$
$$(ab)^3 = a^3 b^3$$
$$(3x^2 y)^3 = 3^3 \bullet (x^2)^3 \bullet y^3 = 27x^6 y^3$$

Rule 3. The exponent of the quotient of two powers of the same base, when the power of the dividend is larger than the power of the divisor, equals the difference between the exponents of the two powers.

$$a^m \div a^n = a^{m-n}$$
$$a^8 \div a^3 = a^{8-3} = a^5$$

Rule 4. The exponent of a power of a power of the same base equals the product of the 2 exponents of the power.

$$(a^m)^n = a^{mn}$$
$$(x^3)^3 = x^9$$
$$(3x^2)^4 = 3^4 \bullet (x^2)^4 = 81x^8$$

Rule 5. *Zero as an exponent*
Any number (except zero itself) raised to the zero power equals 1. Example:
$$a^0 = 1,\ 5^0 = 1,\ (5a)^0 = 1,\ 3a^0 = 3 \bullet 1 = 3.$$

Rule 6. *Negative integral exponents*

$a^{-n} = \dfrac{1}{a^n}$ is the definition of a negative exponent. Examples:

$$a^{-2} = \frac{1}{a^2}$$
$$\frac{x^2}{y^3} = x^2 \bullet y^{-3} = x^2 y^{-3}$$
$$\frac{1}{100} = \frac{1}{10^2} = 10^{-2}$$
$$\frac{a^{-3}}{b^{-2}} = \frac{b^2}{a^3}$$

Fractional Exponents

Fractional exponents establish a link between radicals and powers. The general definition of a fractional exponent is

$$a^{\frac{m}{n}} = \sqrt[n]{a^m}$$

Examples:
$$a^{\frac{1}{2}} = \sqrt[2]{a^1} = \sqrt{a}$$
$$a^{\frac{2}{5}} = \sqrt[5]{a^2}$$
$$27^{\frac{2}{3}} = \sqrt[3]{27^2} = 3^2 = 9$$
$$16^{\frac{5}{4}} = \sqrt[4]{16^5} = 2^5 = 32$$
$$x^{\frac{1}{2}} y^{\frac{1}{2}} = (xy)^{\frac{1}{2}} = \sqrt[2]{(xy)^1} = \sqrt{xy}$$

Slope-Intercept Form of a Linear Equation

A linear equation in **slope-intercept form** is
$$y = mx + b$$
where m represents the slope and b represents the y-intercept.

Example
Find the slope and y-intercept of $2x + 3y = 3$.

Solution
The equation must be rewritten to the form $y = mx + b$. To do this, simplify. Solve the equation for y.

$$2x + 3y = 3$$
$$3y = -2x + 3$$
$$y = -\frac{2}{3}x + \frac{3}{3} \text{ or } y = -\frac{2}{3}x + 1$$

The slope and y-intercepts are $m = -\dfrac{2}{3}$ and $b = 1$.

Example
Find the slope and y-intercept of $y + 5 = 0$.

Solution
This is a special case.
$$y + 5 = 0$$
$$y = -5$$
$$or$$
$$y = 0 \bullet x - 5$$

The slope and *y* intercepts are *m* = 0 (horizontal line)

$$b = -5$$

Example
Find the slope and *y*-intercept of $x - 3 = 0$.

Solution
This is also is special case. Since the equation cannot be solved for *y*, solve it for *x*.

$$x - 3 = 0$$
$$x = 3$$

There is *no slope* since the equation cannot be solved for *y* and there is no *y*-intercept (vertical line). The only information we have, *x* = 3, tells us where the line crosses the *x*-axis (the *x*-intercept). NOTE: The graph is a vertical line.

Parallel and Perpendicular Lines

Parallel lines have the *same* slope.
Perpendicular lines have slopes that are *negative reciprocals* of each other.
When working with parallel and perpendicular lines, it is best to write your equations in the slope-intercept form ($y = mx + b$).

Example
Write the linear equation whose slope and *y*-intercept are 3 and -4, respectively.

Solution
$$y = mx + b$$
(Equation of a line where *m* = slope and *b* = *y*-intercept)

$$\boxed{y = 3x - 4}$$

Substituting *m* = 3 and *b* = 4

Example
Write a linear equation that is parallel to $y = 3x - 4$.

Solution
$$y = 3x - 4$$
$$y = mx + b$$
(Equation of a line)

$$\boxed{y = 3x + 2}$$

The slope of the parallel line equals the slope of the given line. The *y*-intercept may have any value, like 2, which is substituted in the formula. Same slope (3).

Example
Write a linear equation that is perpendicular to $y = 3x - 4$.

Solution
$$y = mx + b \text{ (Equation of a line)}$$

To write the equation of a line that is perpendicular to the given line, substitute the negative reciprocal of the slope of the equation for *m*. The *y*-intercept may have any value; in this case we kept -4.

$$y = 3x - 4$$
$$\boxed{y = -\frac{1}{3}x - 4}$$

Orientation Exercises

1. Solve for x: $2x - 3 > 11$
   A. $x > 4$ D. $x > -7$
   B. $x > 7$ E. $x < -4$
   C. $x < -7$

2. Solve for x: $7 < 2x + 11$
   A. $x < -2$ D. $x < 2$
   B. $x > -2$ E. None of the above
   C. $x > 2$

3.
$$\longleftarrow | \; | \; | \; \oplus | \; | \; | \; | \; | \; | \; \oplus \longrightarrow$$
      -4 -3 -2 -1 0 1 2 3 4   is the graph of:
   A. $|x + 1| < 3$ D. $|x - 1| > 3$
   B. $|x + 3| < 1$ E. $|x - 3| > 1$
   C. $|x - 1| < 3$

4. Solve for x: $|2x - 4| = 10$
   A. $\{-3, -7\}$ D. $\{3, 7\}$
   B. $\{-3, 7\}$ E. $\varnothing$
   C. $\{3, -7\}$

5. Any quantity, not zero, raised to the power zero equals:
   A. -1   D. its reciprocal
   B. 0   E. the quantity itself
   C. 1

6. The fraction $\dfrac{1}{100,000,000}$ can be written as:
   A. 10^7 D. 10^{-7}
   B. 10^8 E. None of the above
   C. 10^{-8}

7. Simplify $8y^{3a + 2b + 2c} \div 2y^{a - 2b + c}$.

   A. $4y^{4a + 3c}$
   B. $4y^{-2a - 4b - c}$
   C. $4y^{2a + 4b + c}$
   D. $4y^{2a - 4b + c}$
   E. None of the above

8. With $x \neq 0$, the expression $5x^0(5x)^0$ is equivalent to:
   A. 0   D. 25
   B. 1   E. $5x$
   C. 5

9. Find the slope of the line with the equation $2x + 3y = -12$.
   A. -4   D. $\dfrac{2}{3}$
   B. -2   E. 3
   C. $-\dfrac{2}{3}$

10. Find the slope of the linear equation $x - 2y = -6$.
    A. -3   D. 1
    B. -1   E. 3
    C. $\dfrac{1}{2}$

11. If the slope of one leg of a right triangle is $\dfrac{1}{2}$, then the slope of the other leg must be:
    A. -2   D. $\dfrac{3}{2}$
    B. $-\dfrac{1}{2}$ E. 2
    C. $\dfrac{1}{2}$

12. If the slope of one leg of a right triangle is 3, then the slope of the other leg must be:
    A. -3   D. $\dfrac{2}{3}$
    B. $-\dfrac{1}{3}$ E. 3
    C. $\dfrac{1}{3}$

Practice Exercises

1. Solve for x: $2 + 3(5 - x) < 8$
   A. $x < 3$
   B. $x > 3$
   C. $x > -9$
   D. $x < -3$
   E. $x > -3$

2. Which of the following inequalities is NOT true when r, s, and t are real numbers?
   A. If $r < 0$, then $\dfrac{1}{r} < 0$.
   B. If $r > s$, then $r + t > s + t$.
   C. If $r > s$ and $s > t$, then $r > t$.
   D. If $r < 0$, then $r^2 < 0$.
   E. If $r > 0$, then $-r < 0$.

3. Solve for x: $|3 - 2x| = 5$
   A. $\{-1, -4\}$
   B. $\{-1, 4\}$
   C. $\{1, 1\}$
   D. $\{1, -1\}$
   E. None of the above

4. The open sentence $|2x - 3| < 7$ is equivalent to which of the following graphs?

   A.

   B.

   C.

   D.

   E.

5. Simplify $-7x^4 \bullet 4x^2$.
   A. $11x^6$
   B. $-11x^8$
   C. $28x^8$
   D. $-28x^6$
   E. $-3x^6$

6. Simplify $\dfrac{36a^2 b^6}{4ab^2}$.
   A. $9ab^3$
   B. $9a^3 b^8$
   C. $9ab^4$
   D. $9a^2 b^{12}$
   E. $40ab^8$

7. Simplify $(2a^3)^3$.
   A. $2a^6$
   B. $2a^9$
   C. $6a^6$
   D. $6a^9$
   E. $8a^9$

8. The expression $8^{-\frac{3}{4}}$ equals:
   A. $-\dfrac{1}{16}$
   B. $\dfrac{1}{16}$
   C. -8
   D. -16
   E. 16

9. The expression $\dfrac{1}{x^4} + \dfrac{2}{x^2 y^2} + \dfrac{1}{y^4}$ is equivalent to:
   A. $\dfrac{1}{x^2} + \dfrac{1}{y^2}$
   B. $\left(\dfrac{1}{x} + \dfrac{1}{y}\right)^2$
   C. $\dfrac{1}{x^2} + \dfrac{\sqrt{2}}{xy} + \dfrac{1}{y^2}$
   D. $(x^{-2} + y^{-2})^2$
   E. None of the above

90

10. Find the *y*-intercept of the line with the equation $2x + y = 5$.

    A. -5
    B. -2
    C. $-\frac{1}{2}$
    D. 0
    E. 5

11. The slope of a line $\frac{1}{2}y = x + 4$ is:

    A. -1
    B. $\frac{1}{2}$
    C. 1
    D. 2
    E. 4

12. What is the slope of a line parallel to the line whose equation is $y = -\frac{1}{2}x + 3$?

    A. -2
    B. $-\frac{1}{2}$
    C. $\frac{1}{2}$
    D. 2
    E. 3

13. What is the slope of a line perpendicular to the line whose equation is $3x - 2y = 0$?

    A. $-\frac{3}{2}$
    B. $-\frac{2}{3}$
    C. $\frac{2}{3}$
    D. $\frac{3}{2}$
    E. No slope

Practice Test

1. Solve for a: $3 - (a - 2) \leq 3 + a$
   - A. $a \leq 1$
   - B. $a \leq -1$
   - C. $a = 1$
   - D. $a \geq 1$
   - E. $a \geq -1$

2. Which of the following is NOT true for all real numbers e, f, and g?
   - A. If $e > 0$, then $\dfrac{1}{e} > 0$.
   - B. If $e < f$, then $eg < fg$.
   - C. If $e < 0$, then $e^2 > 0$.
   - D. If $0 < e < 1$, then $e^2 < e$.
   - E. If $e > 0$, then $-e < 0$.

3. Solve for x: $|x - 4| = 3$.
   - A. $\{1, 7\}$
   - B. $\{1, -7\}$
   - C. $\{-1, 7\}$
   - D. $\{-1, -7\}$
   - E. $\{-7, 7\}$

4. The open sentence $|x + 2| > 5$ is equivalent to which of the open sentences?
   - A. $x + 2 < 5$ or $x + 2 > 5$
   - B. $x + 2 > 5$ and $-5 < x + 2$
   - C. $x + 2 > 5$ or $-5 < x + 2$
   - D. $x + 2 > -5$ or $5 < x + 2$
   - E. $x + 2 > -5$ and $x + 2 < 5$

5. Simplify 4^0.
   - A. 4
   - B. -4
   - C. 0
   - D. 1
   - E. -1

6. Simplify $4a^0$.
   - A. 4
   - B. -4
   - C. 0
   - D. 1
   - E. -1

7. Simplify $(4a)^0$.
   - A. 4
   - B. -4
   - C. 0
   - D. 1
   - E. -1

8. Write $\dfrac{3^{-2}}{4^{-2}}$ without negative exponents.
   - A. 1
   - B. .75
   - C. $\dfrac{8}{3}$
   - D. $\dfrac{16}{9}$
   - E. $\dfrac{9}{16}$

9. The expression $\left(\dfrac{a}{a^{-2}}\right)^{\frac{1}{2}}$ where $a \neq 0$ equals:
   - A. $-a$
   - B. $a^{\frac{1}{2}}$
   - C. $a^{\frac{3}{2}}$
   - D. a
   - E. None of the above

10. Simplify $64^{-\frac{2}{3}} \cdot 8^{\frac{4}{3}}$.
    - A. -1
    - B. 0
    - C. 1
    - D. 16
    - E. 64

11. Find the slope of the line with the equation
    $$y - 1{,}000 = 0.$$
    - A. -1
    - B. 0
    - C. 1
    - D. 1,000
    - E. No slope

12. Which of the following lines does NOT have a slope equal to $\frac{2}{3}$?

    A. $2x - 3y = 0$
    B. $3y = 12 + 2x$
    C. $2x + 3y = 9$
    D. $\dfrac{x}{6} - \dfrac{y}{4} = 5$
    E.   None of the above

13. Find an equation of the line that passes through (2, -3) and is perpendicular to the line $2x - y = 10$.

    A. $x + 2y = -4$
    B. $x + 2y = 8$
    C. $x - 2y = 4$
    D. $x + 2y = -8$
    E. $x - 2y = 5$

14. Which of the following pairs of equations are perpendicular?

    A. $y = 3x - 3$
        $y = \dfrac{1}{3}x + 2$
    B. $y = 5 - 4x$
        $y = 5 + 4x$
    C. $y = 3$
        $y = -\dfrac{1}{3}$
    D. $2x + 3y = 0$
        $2x - 3y = 0$
    E. $6x - 3y = 12$
        $x + 2y = 10$

Systems of Two Linear Equations with Two Variables

If there are two unknown quantities in a problem, two equations are needed to find their values. To do this, you must eliminate one of the variables.

In this section we will show you an algebraic solution for a system of equations.

Example
Solve the following system of equations
$$x + 3y = 7$$
$$2x - 3y = 8$$

Solution
Inspection of the two equations indicates that y can be eliminated by addition.

$$
\begin{array}{rl}
x + 3y = & 7 \\
2x - 3y = & 8 \\
\hline
3x \quad\quad = & 15
\end{array}
$$

(Add)
(Solve for x) $\qquad\qquad x = 5$
(Substitute in the first equation) $\quad 5 + 3y = 7$
$$3y = 2$$

(Solve for y) $\qquad\qquad\qquad y = \dfrac{2}{3}$

$$x = 5 \text{ and } y = \frac{2}{3}$$

NOTE: The graphical solution would be 1 point of intersection at $\left(5, \dfrac{2}{3}\right)$.

Example
Solve the system $\quad 2x - 2y = 5$
$$-x + y = -1$$

Solution
Inspection of the two equations indicates that x can be eliminated if we multiply the second equation by 2 and add.
(Rewrite equation 1)
(Multiply equation 2 by 2)

$$
\begin{array}{rl}
2x - 2y = & 5 \\
-2x + 2y = & -2 \\
\hline
0 = & 3
\end{array}
$$

Both variables x and y are eliminated and we are left with the statement $0 = 3$, which is false. There is no solution to this problem. The solution set is represented by $\{\ \}$.

NOTE: The graphical depiction of this problem would show that the lines are parallel and there is no intersection.

Rational Expressions

A rational algebraic expression is a quotient of polynomials. Here are some examples:
$$\frac{5xy^2}{3w}, \ \frac{a^2 - 5a + 4}{a^2 + 9}, \ x^2(x-2)^{-2} = \frac{x^2}{(x-2)^2}$$
A rational algebraic expression is expressed in its simplest form when it is reduced to lowest terms.

Example
Reduce $\dfrac{-6a^2 b}{2ab^2 c}$.

Solution
$$\frac{-6a^2 b}{2ab^2 c} = \frac{-3 \bullet 2 \bullet a \bullet a \bullet b}{2 \bullet a \bullet b \bullet b \bullet c} = \frac{-3a}{bc}$$

Example
Reduce $(3x^2 - 3)(2x + 2)^{-1}$.

Solution
$(3x^2 - 3)(2x + 2)^{-1}$

(Rewrite as fraction) $\qquad = \dfrac{3x^2 - 3}{2x + 2}$

(Factor the numerator and denominator)
$$= \frac{3(x+1)(x-1)}{2(x+1)}$$

(Divide by $x + 1$) $\qquad = \dfrac{3(x-1)}{2}$

Example
Reduce $(1 - x)(x^2 - 1)^{-1}$.

Solution

$(1-x)(x^2-1)^{-1}$

(Rewrite as fraction) $\quad = \dfrac{1-x}{x^2-1}$

(Factor) $\quad = \dfrac{(-1)(-1+x)}{(x+1)(x-1)}$

(Recall $1-x = -1(x-1)$) $\quad = \dfrac{-1}{x+1}$

Example

Find the product $\left(\dfrac{2}{3x-9}\right)\left(\dfrac{x^2-9}{4x-1}\right)$.

Solution

$$\dfrac{2}{3(\cancel{x-3})} \bullet \dfrac{\overset{1}{\cancel{(x-3)}}(x+3)}{4x-1}$$

$$\dfrac{2(x+3)}{3(4x-1)}$$

Example

Find the quotient $\dfrac{4x^2-4}{3x+6} \div \dfrac{2x+2}{x^2-4}$.

Solution

(Factor) $\qquad \dfrac{4(x^2-1)}{3(x+2)} \div \dfrac{2(x+1)}{(x+2)(x-2)}$

(Multiply by reciprocal)

$$\dfrac{\overset{2}{\cancel{4}}\overset{1}{\cancel{(x+1)}}(x-1)}{3\cancel{(x+2)}} \times \dfrac{\overset{1}{\cancel{(x+2)}}(x-2)}{2\cancel{(x+1)}}$$

$$\dfrac{2(x-1)(x-2)}{3}$$

Example

Find the sum $\dfrac{3}{x+2} + \dfrac{4}{x+2}$.

Solution

Since the denominators are alike, add the numerators and keep the denominator.

$$\dfrac{3+4}{x+2} = \dfrac{7}{x+2}$$

Example

Find the sum $\dfrac{4}{x-1} + \dfrac{3}{x^2-1}$.

Solution

Factor the denominator:

$$= \dfrac{4}{x-1} + \dfrac{3}{(x-1)(x+1)}$$

Since the LCD is $(x+1)(x-1)$, multiply the first fraction by $\dfrac{x+1}{x+1}$:

$$= \dfrac{4(x+1)}{(x-1)(x+1)} + \dfrac{3}{(x-1)(x+1)}$$

Add the numerators:

$$= \dfrac{4(x+1)+3}{(x-1)(x+1)}$$

Combine terms:

$$= \dfrac{4x+4+3}{(x-1)(x+1)}$$

$$= \dfrac{4x+7}{(x+1)(x-1)}$$

Example

Find the difference $\dfrac{5}{6x} - \dfrac{2x-5}{3x^2}$.

Solution

Since the LCD is $6x^2$, multiply the first fraction by $\dfrac{x}{x}$ and the second by $\dfrac{2}{2}$:

$$= \dfrac{x}{x} \bullet \dfrac{5}{6x} - \dfrac{2}{2} \bullet \dfrac{2x-5}{3x^2}$$

$$= \dfrac{5x}{6x^2} - \dfrac{2(2x-5)}{6x^2}$$

Combine the numerators:

$$= \dfrac{5x-2(2x-5)}{6x^2}$$

$$= \dfrac{5x-4x+10}{6x^2} = \dfrac{x+10}{6x^2}$$

Simplification and Operations with Radicals and the Imaginary Unit

It is customary to write a radical in its reduced form.

Example

Simplify $\sqrt{90}$.

Solution

$\sqrt{90} = \sqrt{9}\sqrt{10} = 3\sqrt{10}$

The next step in your work with radicals is to develop rules of procedure for multiplying, dividing, adding, and subtracting radicals.

Example

Simplify $2\sqrt{3} \bullet 5\sqrt{12}$.

Solution

Multiply the coefficients and the radicands, then simplify the resulting radical.

$2\sqrt{3} \bullet 5\sqrt{12} = 10\sqrt{36} = 10 \bullet 6 = 60$

Example

$5\sqrt{3}\left(\sqrt{3} - \sqrt{5}\right)$.

Solution

Multiply each term inside the parenthesis by the monomial and then simplify.

$5\sqrt{3}\left(\sqrt{3} - \sqrt{5}\right) = 5\sqrt{9} - 5\sqrt{15} = 5 \bullet 3 - 5\sqrt{15} =$
$15 - 5\sqrt{15}$

The division of two radicals of the same order uses a principle that leads to the same result as that obtained by using simple division of the value of the radicals.

Example

$\dfrac{\sqrt{81}}{\sqrt{9}} = \dfrac{9}{3} = 3$ or $\dfrac{\sqrt{81}}{\sqrt{9}} = \sqrt{\dfrac{81}{9}} = \sqrt{9} = 3$.

However, when two radicals are divided, the result must be left in such a form that the denominator does not contain a radical.

Example

Divide $\sqrt{2}$ by $\sqrt{3}$.

Solution

$\dfrac{\sqrt{2}}{\sqrt{3}} = \sqrt{\dfrac{2}{3}}$

The result still has 3 under the radical sign in the denominator. The denominator can be made a perfect square by multiplying the numerator and the denominator of the radicand by $\sqrt{3}$.

$$\frac{\sqrt{2}}{\sqrt{3}} = \frac{\sqrt{2}}{\sqrt{3}} \bullet \frac{\sqrt{3}}{\sqrt{3}} = \frac{\sqrt{6}}{\sqrt{9}} = \frac{\sqrt{6}}{3}$$

Example

Simplify $\dfrac{\sqrt{3}}{\sqrt{5} + \sqrt{2}}$

Solution

This example contains a binomial in the denominator. To obtain a denominator containing no radical sign entails the multiplying of the numerator and denominator by $\sqrt{5} - \sqrt{2}$. The sum of two quantities multiplied by their difference is equal to the square of the first minus the square of the second.

$$\frac{\sqrt{3}}{\sqrt{5} + \sqrt{2}} = \frac{\sqrt{3}}{\sqrt{5} + \sqrt{2}} \bullet \frac{\sqrt{5} - \sqrt{2}}{\sqrt{5} - \sqrt{2}}$$
$$= \frac{\sqrt{3}\left(\sqrt{5} - \sqrt{2}\right)}{\left(\sqrt{5}\right)^2 - \left(\sqrt{2}\right)^2} = \frac{\sqrt{15} - \sqrt{6}}{5 - 2} = \frac{\sqrt{15} - \sqrt{6}}{3}$$

The process of dividing two radicals is called **rationalizing the denominator**.

If the radicals in an expression have the same index and same radicand, they can be combined by adding their coefficients in the same way that similar terms can be combined. Just as $4a + 5a = 9a$, $4\sqrt{2} + 5\sqrt{2} = 9\sqrt{2}$. On the other hand, terms like $\sqrt{3}$ and $\sqrt{5}$ cannot be combined because the radicands are different.

Example

Simplify $3\sqrt{3} - \sqrt{3} + 2\sqrt{3}$.

Solution

Since the terms have identical indices and radicands, they can be combined immediately.

$3\sqrt{3} - \sqrt{3} + 2\sqrt{3} = 4\sqrt{3}$

Example

Simplify $\sqrt{90} - 3\sqrt{40} + 3\sqrt{160}$.

Solution

In this expression, the radicals have the same index but different radicands. First simplify the radicals and perhaps there will be radicals that can be combined.

$\sqrt{90} - 3\sqrt{40} + 3\sqrt{160}$

$\sqrt{9}\sqrt{10} - 3 \bullet \sqrt{4}\sqrt{10} + 3 \bullet \sqrt{16}\sqrt{10}$

$3\sqrt{10} - 3 \bullet 2\sqrt{10} + 3 \bullet 4\sqrt{10}$

$3\sqrt{10} - 6\sqrt{10} + 12\sqrt{10} = 9\sqrt{10}$

The Imaginary Unit

An imaginary number is an even root of a negative number. The definition of an imaginary unit is:

$i = \sqrt{-1}$ so that $i^2 = -1$

The principles developed for the operations of addition, subtraction, multiplication, and division with radicals apply to imaginary numbers.

Example

Express in terms of i: $\sqrt{-16}$

Solution

$\sqrt{-16} = \sqrt{16}\sqrt{-1} = 4i$

Example

Express in terms of i: $3\sqrt{-4}$

Solution

$3\sqrt{-4} = 3 \bullet \sqrt{4}\sqrt{-1} = 3 \bullet 2i = 6i$

Example

Express $5\sqrt{-36} - 2\sqrt{-36}$ as one term.

Solution

Extract the i:

$= 5i\sqrt{36} - 2i\sqrt{36}$
$= 5i \bullet 6 - 2i \bullet 6$
$= 30i - 12i$
$= 18i$

Example

Multiply $\sqrt{-5}$ by $\sqrt{-15}$.

Solution

Express each radical in terms of i:

$\sqrt{-5} \bullet \sqrt{-15} = i\sqrt{5} \bullet i\sqrt{15}$

$\qquad = i^2\sqrt{75}$ (Remember $i^2 = -1$)

$\qquad = -\sqrt{25}\sqrt{3}$

$\qquad = -5\sqrt{3}$

NOTE: The imaginary unit has the special property that successive powers run through a cycle of values.

$i = \sqrt{-1}$
$i^2 = -1$
$i^3 = i^2 \bullet i^1 = -i$
$i^4 = i^2 \bullet i^2 = 1$
$i^5 = i^4 \bullet i^1 = 1 \bullet i = i$
$i^6 = i^4 \bullet i^2 = 1 \bullet (-1) = -1$
$i^7 = i^4 \bullet i^3 = 1 \bullet (-i) = -i$
$i^8 = i^4 \bullet i^4 = 1 \bullet 1 = 1$

Any power of i that is an exact multiple of 4 is equal to 1. Thus,

$i^{21} = i^{20} \bullet i = i$

A complex number is a number that has the form $a + bi$, where a and b are real numbers.

Example

Add $-3 + 5i$ and $7 - 11i$.

Solution

Find the sum of the real parts and the sum of the imaginary parts:

$(-3 + 5i) + (7 - 11i) = 4 - 6i$

Example

Find the product $(3 - 5i)(5 + 4i)$.

Solution

The product of two complex numbers will be a complex number:

$(3 - 5i)(5 + 4i)$
$= 15 - 25i + 12i - 20i^2$
$= 15 - 13i + 20$
$= 35 - 13i$

Quadratic Formula

The quadratic formula is derived by solving a quadratic equation in standard form by completing the square. The two roots of the equation $ax^2 + bx + c = 0$ are

$$x = \frac{-b + \sqrt{b^2 - 4ac}}{2a} \text{ and } x = \frac{-b - \sqrt{b^2 - 4ac}}{2a}$$

Memorize these formulas and you will be able to use them in solving any quadratic (second degree) equation.

Example
Solve the equation $3x^2 - 12x + 5 = 0$

Solution
The equation must be in standard form (equal to zero). The coefficient of the x-squared term is a, the coefficient of the linear term is b, and the constant term is c. Hence, $a = 3$, $b = -12$, $c = 5$.

Using the quadratic formula
$$x = \frac{-b \pm \sqrt{b^2 - 4ac}}{2a}$$
(Substitute the values of a, b, and c)
$$x = \frac{-12 \pm \sqrt{144 - 4(3)(5)}}{2(3)}$$
(Simplify)
$$x = \frac{-12 \pm \sqrt{144 - 60}}{6}$$
$$x = \frac{-12 \pm \sqrt{84}}{6}$$
$$x = \frac{-12 \pm 2\sqrt{21}}{6}$$
(Divide by 2)
$$x = \frac{-6 \pm \sqrt{21}}{3}$$

Observe that the value of $b^2 - 4ac$, the radicand in the formula $x = \dfrac{-b \pm \sqrt{b^2 - 4ac}}{2a}$ indicates the sort of roots to expect.

If $b^2 - 4ac > 0$, there are two real roots.
If $b^2 - 4ac = 0$, there is one real root (called a double root).
If $b^2 - 4ac < 0$, there are two conjugate imaginary roots.

Zeros of Polynomials

Any value, or values, of x that satisfy an equation are called the roots (or solutions, or **zeros**) of the equation. By setting y equal to the function and plotting, we get a polynomial curve.

The x-coordinates of the point or points, if they exist, at which the curve crosses the x-axis are called x-intercepts or the **zeros of the function**.

The remainder theorem and the factor theorem enable us to factor some polynomials that do not yield to any previously mentioned factoring methods.

The polynomial $x^2 - x - 12$ is a function of x, since its value depends upon the value of x. The words "function of x" may be abbreviated $f(x)$. This isn't just any "function of x"; it is the specific function with the name f.

If $f(x) = x^2 - x - 12$, then $f(2)$, the value of the function when $x = 2$, is found by substituting 2 for x in the polynomial, and f(-2) is found by substituting -2 for x in the polynomial.

Look at the following results

$$(x^2 - x - 12) \div (x + 2) = x - 3 + \frac{-6}{x + 2}$$
$$f(x) = x^2 - x - 12$$
$$f(-2) = 4 + 2 - 12 = -6$$

$$(x^2 - x - 12) \div (x - 2) = x + 1 + \frac{-10}{x - 2}$$
$$f(2) = 4 - 2 - 12 = -10$$

$$(x^2 - x - 12) \div (x + 3) = x - 4 + \frac{0}{x + 3}$$
$$f(-3) = 9 - 3 - 12 = 0$$

Compare the three remainders with the three values of the polynomial; these observations illustrate the **remainder theorem**.

If $f(x)$ is divided by $x - a$, remainder $= f(a)$.

Notice that there is a remainder of 0 when $x^2 - x - 12$ is divided by $x + 3$.

This observation brings us to the **factor theorem**, which states if a polynomial in x equals zero when a is substituted for x, then $x - a$ is a factor of the polynomial or

if $f(a) = 0$, $x - a$ is a factor of $f(x)$.

Example

Factor $x^3 + x^2 + 4$, using the factor theorem.

Solution

If $x^3 + x^2 + 4$ has a factor of the type $x - a$, then a is an exact divisor of 4. The possibilities for a are +1, -1, +2, -2, +4, -4.

$f(x) = x^3 + x^2 + 4$
$f(1) = 1 + 1 + 4 = 6$
$f(-1) = -1 + 1 + 4 = 4$
$f(2) = 8 + 4 + 4 = 16$
$f(-2) = -8 + 4 + 4 = 0$ then $x + 2$ is an exact divisor of $x^3 + x^2 + 4$.
By division $x^3 + x^2 + 4 = (x + 2)(x^2 - x + 2)$

Thus, the zeros of the function $f(x)$ are the roots of the equation $f(x) = 0$.

Orientation Exercises

1. Which of the following systems of equations does NOT have a solution?
   - A. $2x + 4y = 26$
     $2x - 4y = 10$
   - B. $2x - 4y = 10$
     $4x + 2y = 14$
   - C. $2x + 4y = 10$
     $4x - 2y = 14$
   - D. $2x - 4y = 10$
     $4x - 8y = 14$
   - E. $2x + 4y = 26$
     $4x - 2y = 14$

2. Solve the following system: $\dfrac{1}{x} + \dfrac{1}{y} = \dfrac{5}{6}$
   $\dfrac{1}{x} - \dfrac{1}{y} = \dfrac{1}{6}$
   - A. $x = 3$ and $y = -2$
   - B. $x = 2$ and $y = 3$
   - C. $x = 3$ and $y = 2$
   - D. $x = -2$ and $y = -3$
   - E. None of the above

3. For all $x \neq 0$ and $y \neq 0$, $\dfrac{\left(4x^{-2}y^3\right)^2}{xy} = ?$
   - A. $\dfrac{4y^4}{x^2}$
   - B. $\dfrac{9y^4}{x^2}$
   - C. $\dfrac{9y^7}{x^5}$
   - D. $9x^3y^8$
   - E. $\dfrac{16y^5}{x^5}$

4. Simplify $\sqrt{32}$.
   - A. $2\sqrt{8}$
   - B. $2\sqrt{4}$
   - C. $4\sqrt{2}$
   - D. $3\sqrt{4}$
   - E. 6

5. Which of these is an irrational number?
   - A. $\sqrt{16}$
   - B. $3\sqrt{25}$
   - C. $\sqrt{\dfrac{4}{9}}$
   - D. $\sqrt{6}$
   - E. $\dfrac{\sqrt{3}}{\sqrt{27}}$

6. One solution for the equation $3x^2 + 2x - 4 = 0$ is $\dfrac{-1-\sqrt{13}}{3}$. What is the other solution?
   - A. $\dfrac{-1-\sqrt{13}}{3}$
   - B. $\dfrac{1-\sqrt{13}}{3}$
   - C. $-\dfrac{1}{3} + \sqrt{13}$
   - D. $\dfrac{-1+\sqrt{13}}{3}$
   - E. $-1 + \dfrac{\sqrt{13}}{3}$

7. One solution for the equation $y^2 - 4y + 2 = 0$ is $2 + \sqrt{2}$. What is the other solution?
   - A. $-2 - \sqrt{2}$
   - B. $2 + 2\sqrt{2}$
   - C. $2 - \sqrt{2}$
   - D. $2 + \sqrt{2}$
   - E. None of the above

8. Find the zeros of the function
   $$f(x) = x^2 - 3x - 10.$$
   - A. $10, -1$
   - B. $-10, 1$
   - C. $5, -2$
   - D. $-5, 2$
   - E. None of the above

Practice Exercises

1. Solve the following system: $a - 12b = 5$
$$2a - 10b = 66$$
   A. $a = -53$ and $b = -4$
   B. $a = 53$ and $b = -4$
   C. $a = -53$ and $b = 4$
   D. $a = 53$ and $b = 4$
   E. None of the above

2. If $3x + 2y = 13$ and $2x + 3y = 12$, find the value of $x - y$.
   A. 1
   B. 2
   C. 3
   D. 5
   E. 6

3. Simplify $\dfrac{x+3}{x-2} \bullet \dfrac{2x-4}{2}$.
   A. $x - 3$
   B. $x + 3$
   C. $x - 2$
   D. $x + 2$
   E. $\dfrac{x+3}{x-2}$

4. $\sqrt{48}$ divided by which of the following numbers yields a rational number?
   A. $\sqrt{2}$
   B. $\sqrt{4}$
   C. $\sqrt{6}$
   D. $\sqrt{12}$
   E. $\sqrt{16}$

5. $\left(\sqrt{2}+\sqrt{6}\right)^2 + \left(\sqrt{3}-\sqrt{4}\right)^2 = ?$
   A. 7
   B. $7 + 8\sqrt{3}$
   C. 13
   D. 15
   E. None of the above

6. Convert $\sqrt{-50}$ to i notation.
   A. $-50i$
   B. $2i\sqrt{5}$
   C. $5i\sqrt{2}$
   D. $2i$
   E. $5i$

7. For what value of k will the equation $x^2 - 4x + k = 0$ have only one distinct real solution for x?
   A. -4
   B. -2
   C. 0
   D. 4
   E. 16

8. The equation $y^2 + 2y - 2 = 0$ has a root of:
   A. -3
   B. 3
   C. $-1 + \sqrt{3}$
   D. $\sqrt{3} - 1$
   E. $\sqrt{2}$

9. Find the zeros of the function
$$f(x) = 2x^2 + 3x - 5.$$
   A. -5
   B. -5, 1
   C. 5, -1
   D. $-\dfrac{5}{2}$, 1
   E. $\dfrac{5}{2}$, -1

10. Which of the following is a factor of
$$x^5 + 32?$$
   A. $x + 1$
   B. $x - 1$
   C. $x + 2$
   D. $x - 2$
   E. $x + 3$

Practice Test

1. The sum of the reciprocals of two numbers is $\frac{8}{15}$ and the difference of their reciprocals is $\frac{2}{15}$. What are the numbers?

   A. $3, \frac{3}{19}$ D. $\frac{3}{2}, -\frac{5}{6}$

   B. $3, 5$ E. None of the above

   C. $3, \frac{5}{8}$

2. Solve the following system: $3x - y = 11$
   $x + y = 5$

   A. $x = 4$ and $y = 1$
   B. $x = 4$ and $y = -1$
   C. $x = -4$ and $y = 1$
   D. $x = -4$ and $y = -1$
   E. None of the above

3. Write the expression $-15(5x - 15)^{-1}$ as a fraction in lowest terms.

   A. $\frac{3}{x-3}$ D. $\frac{-3}{x+3}$

   B. $\frac{3}{x+3}$ E. $\frac{-1}{x}$

   C. $\frac{-3}{x-3}$

4. For all positive x and y, $\sqrt{24x^9 y^3} = ?$

   A. $2x^4 y\sqrt{6xy}$

   B. $2x^4 y\sqrt{12xy}$

   C. $6x^4 y\sqrt{2xy}$

   D. $4x^4 y\sqrt{6xy}$

   E. $4x^3 y\sqrt{y}$

5. Evaluate i^{38}.
   A. i
   B. -1
   C. $-i$
   D. 1
   E. $\sqrt{-1}$

6. Find the product $(3i + 5)(3i - 2)$.

   A. $-19 + 9i$
   B. -19
   C. $-6 + 9i$
   D. $-19 + 21i$
   E. $3 + 6i$

7. What is the reciprocal of $3 + i$?

   A. $\frac{3-i}{8}$ D. $-3 - i$

   B. $\frac{3-i}{8}$ E. $\frac{3-i}{10}$

   C. $3 - i$

8. For what value of k will the equation $n^2 + 6n + k = 0$ have only one distinct real solution for n?

   A. 36 D. -6
   B. 9 E. -9
   C. 0

9. For what value of k will the equation $4x^2 - 12x + k = 0$ have only one distinct real solution for x?

   A. -12 D. 9
   B. -6 E. 36
   C. 0

10. Find the zeros of the function $f(x) = x^2 - 5x + 6$.

    A. $-6, 1$
    B. $3, -2$
    C, $-3, 2$
    D. $3, 2$
    E. $-3, -2$

11. Which of the following is a factor of $2x^3 - 5x^2 - 6x + 9$?

    A. $x + 1$
    B. $x - 1$
    C. $x + 3$
    D. $x - 3$
    E. $x + 6$

COORDINATE GEOMETRY
SKILL BUILDER NINE

Graphing on the Number Line

Every real number can be graphed as a point on a number line.

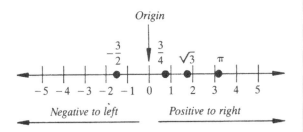

Familiarize yourself with these sets of numbers and their graphs.

Example

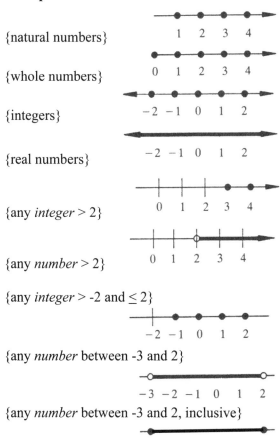

{natural numbers}

{whole numbers}

{integers}

{real numbers}

{any *integer* > 2}

{any *number* > 2}

{any *integer* > -2 and ≤ 2}

{any *number* between -3 and 2}

{any *number* between -3 and 2, inclusive}

{any *number* greater than -1 and less than or equal to 3, except 0}

{any integer between 1 and 2}

Graphs of Functions and Relations in the Standard Coordinate Plane

A **relation** is any set of ordered pairs of numbers. The set of first coordinates in the ordered pair is the **domain**, and the set of second coordinates is the **range**.

Example
Graph the relation.
{(0, 0), (1, 2), (1, -2), (4, 4), (4, -4), (3, 6)}
State the domain and range.

Solution

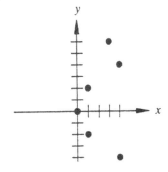

Domain = {0, 1, 3, 4}
Range = {-4, -2, 0, 2, 4, 6}

A **function** is a special kind of relation.
A **function** is a relation in which each element in the domain corresponds to a unique element in the range.

NOTE: Different number pairs never have the same first coordinate.

Example

$\{(1, 4), (4, 8), (5, 8), (8, 9)\}$ is an example of a function.

Domain = $\{1, 4, 5, 8\}$

Range = $\{4, 8, 9\}$

No vertical line intersects the graph of a function in more than 1 point.

Example

Are the following graphs of functions?

I. Function   **II. Function**

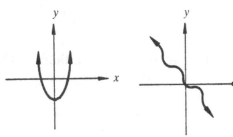

III. Not a Function   **IV. Function**

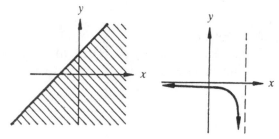

III is not a function because a vertical line intersects at an infinite number of points within the shaded region. I, II, and IV all pass the vertical line test.

The notation $f(x) = x^2 + 5x + 6$ is also used to name a function. To find $f(0)$ means substitute 0 for x in $f(x)$.

Example

$f(x) = x^2 + 5x - 4$

$f(0) = 0^2 + 5 \bullet 0 - 4 = -4$

$f(2) = 2^2 + 5 \bullet 2 - 4 = 10$

$f(a) = a^2 + 5a - 4$

Example

If $f(x) = x^2 + 5$ and $g(x) = 1 + x$, find $g(f(2))$.

Solution

First find $f(2)$ $f(2) = 2^2 + 5$

$f(2) = 4 + 5$

$f(2) = 9$

Next find $g(f(2)) = g(9)$

$g(9) = 1 + 9$

$g(9) = 10$

Slope of a Line

The slope of a line is its steepness or tilt. A vertical line is not tilted, therefore it has *no* slope. A horizontal line has a slope of zero.

$$\text{slope} = m = \frac{\text{Vertical change}}{\text{Horizontal change}} =$$

$$\frac{\text{difference of } y\text{'s}}{\text{difference of } x\text{'s}} = \frac{y_2 - y_1}{x_2 - x_1}, (x_2 \neq x_1)$$

Example

If given the graph of a line the slope can be determined by finding $\dfrac{\text{rise}}{\text{run}}$.

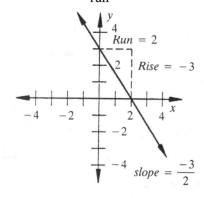

$Run = 2$

$Rise = -3$

$slope = \dfrac{-3}{2}$

Example

If given two points of a line the slope can be found by finding

$(0, 3) (2, 0)$

$$\text{slope} = \frac{3 - 0}{0 - 2} = \frac{3}{-2} = \frac{-3}{2}$$

$$\frac{\text{difference of } y\text{'s}}{\text{difference of } x\text{'s}} = \frac{y_2 - y_1}{x_2 - x_1}, (x_2 \neq x_1)$$

104

Example

If given the equation of a line, transform it into the form $y = mx + b$ where m represents the slope.

$3x + 2y = 6$

$2y = -3x + 6$

$y = -\dfrac{3}{2}x + 3$

m (coefficient of x term) $= \dfrac{-3}{2}$

Distance Formula for Points in a Plane

The distance (d) between any two points A (x_1, y_1) and B (x_2, y_2) is found by using the formula:

$d = \sqrt{(x_1 - x_2)^2 + (y_1 - y_2)^2}$ or, in other words

$d = \sqrt{(\text{diff. of } x\text{'s})^2 + (\text{diff. of } y\text{'s})^2}$

Example

Find the distance between the points $(7, 9)$ and $(1, 1)$.

Solution

$$d = \sqrt{(7-1)^2 + (9-1)^2}$$
$$= \sqrt{6^2 + 8^2}$$
$$= \sqrt{36 + 64}$$
$$= \sqrt{100}$$
$$= 10$$

Also important is the formula for finding the midpoint of a line segment.

$$\text{Midpoint} = \left(\frac{\text{sum of the } x\text{'s}}{2}, \frac{\text{sum of the } y\text{'s}}{2} \right)$$

Example

The coordinates of the midpoint of the segment whose endpoints are $(7, 9)$ and $(1, 1)$.

$$\text{Midpoint} = \left(\frac{7+1}{2}, \frac{9+1}{2} \right)$$
$$= \left(\frac{8}{2}, \frac{10}{2} \right)$$
$$= (4, 5)$$

Orientation Exercises

1. The diagram represents the graph of what set of numbers?

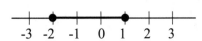

   A. {Integers ≥ -2 and ≤ 1}
   B. {Numbers > -2 and < 1}
   C. {Numbers between -2 and 1}
   D. {Integers between -2 and 1, inclusive}
   E. {Numbers between -2 and 1, inclusive}

2. Which of the following sets represents a function?
   A. {(0, 1), (1, 2), (3, 4), (5, 6), (5, 7)}
   B. {(3, 4), (4, 4), (5, 4)}
   C. {(1, 3), (5, 2), (1, -3), (5, -2)}
   D. {(5, 8), (7, 2), (5, 10)}
   E. None of the above

3. Which of the following represents a function?

   A.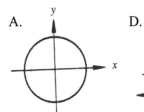

   B.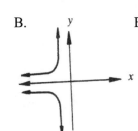

   C.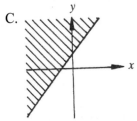

   D.

   E.

4. What is the slope of the line joining (-4, 7) and (-5, 0)?
   A. 7
   B. $\dfrac{1}{7}$
   C. -7
   D. $\dfrac{-9}{7}$
   E. $\dfrac{7}{9}$

5. The slope of a horizontal line is:
   A. -1
   B. 0
   C. 1
   D. 100
   E. No slope

6. How far is the point (-3, -4) from the origin?
   A. $2\sqrt{3}$
   B. $\sqrt{17}$
   C. $\sqrt{22}$
   D. 5
   E. 7

7. The distance from (5, 2) to (1, -1) is:
   A. $\sqrt{5}$
   B. $\sqrt{17}$
   C. 5
   D. $\sqrt{37}$
   E. 9

8. What is the length of the diagonal of the square whose vertices are R (2, 2), S (2, -2), T (-2, -2), and U (-2, 2)?
   A. 4
   B. 6
   C. 8
   D. 10
   E. None of the above

Practice Exercises

1. The figure represents the graph of what set of numbers?

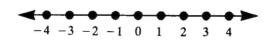

   A. {natural numbers}
   B. {whole numbers}
   C. {integers}
   D. {rational numbers}
   E. {real numbers}

2. The figure represents the graph of what set of numbers?

   A. {natural numbers}
   B. {whole numbers}
   C. {integers}
   D. {rational numbers}
   E. {real numbers}

3. Which of the following represents the range of {(0, -5) (-1, 3) (1, 2) (2, 2) (3, -1) (-5, 3)}?
   A. {-5, -1, 0, 1, 2, 3}
   B. {-1, 0, 3}
   C. {-5, -2, -1, 2}
   D. {-5, -1, 2, 3}
   E. {-5, -1, 0, 2, 3}

4. If $f(x) = x^3 - 1$, then $f(-2) = ?$

   A. -27   D. -1
   B. -9   E. 9
   C. -7

5. The slope of the line whose equation is $4x + 5y = 20$ is ?

   A. $\dfrac{4}{5}$ D. -4

   B. $-\dfrac{4}{5}$ E. $\dfrac{5}{4}$

   C. 4

6. What is the slope of the line joining (5, -2) and (3, -6)?
   A. $-\dfrac{1}{4}$ D. -4

   B. 2   E. 4
   C. -2

7. What is the distance between the points (2, -4) and (-5, 3)?

   A. $7\sqrt{2}$ D. 14
   B. 5   E. 98
   C. $2\sqrt{7}$

8. What is the length of $\overline{AB}$?

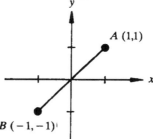

   A. $\sqrt{2}$ D. 1
   B. $\sqrt{3}$ E. 2
   C. $\sqrt{8}$

9. What is the midpoint of $\overline{AB}$?

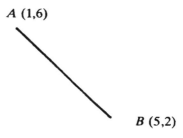

   A. (6, 8)   D. (8, 6)
   B. (3, 4)   E. (3, 1)
   C. (4, 3)

Practice Test

1. The figure represents the graph of what set of numbers?

   A. {natural numbers}
   B. {whole numbers}
   C. {integers}
   D. {rational numbers}
   E. {real numbers}

2. Which of the following number lines represents all numbers x such that $-2 \leq x \leq 2$?

   A.

   B.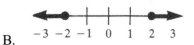

   C.

   D.

   E.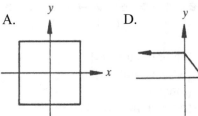

3. Which of the following represents a function?

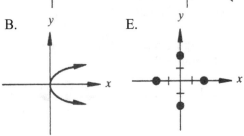

   A.

   B.

   C.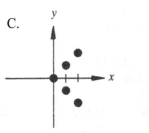

   D.

   E.

4. If $f(x) = x^2 - 5$ and $g(x) = 1 + x$, find $f(g(-2))$.

   A. -4
   B. 0
   C. 2
   D. 4
   E. 10

5. The slope of a vertical line is ?

   A. -1
   B. 0
   C. 1
   D. 100
   E. No slope

108

6. The slope of the line whose equation is
$3x - 5y = 15$ is ?

A. -3
B. 3
C. $\dfrac{-5}{3}$
D. $\dfrac{-3}{5}$
E. $\dfrac{3}{5}$

7. What is the length of line segment AB ?

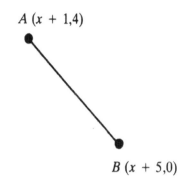

A. $4\sqrt{2}$
B. 4
C. $3\sqrt{2}$
D. 6
E. $8\sqrt{2}$

8. The vertices of a triangle have coordinates as indicated in the standard (x, y) coordinate plane. What is the area of the triangle in square units?

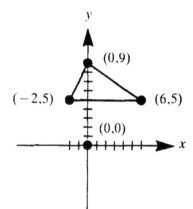

A. 4
B. 16
C. 20
D. 32
E. 36

9. Point P (0, 3) is the center of a circle. Point R (-2, 6) is 1 endpoint of diameter $\overline{RS}$ of this circle. What are the coordinates of point S?

A. (-2, 3)
B. (2, 0)
C. $(-1, 4\dfrac{1}{2})$
D. (-2, 0)
E. (2, 12)

Graphs of Linear Equations with Two Variables

A first degree equation is called a linear equation, since its graph is a straight line. In a linear equation, each term is a constant or a monomial of the first degree.

Example

$2x + 3y = 6$	Linear (first degree)
$y = x^3 - 1$	Not linear (3rd degree)
$xy = 4$	Not linear (2nd degree)
$x + \dfrac{2}{x} = y$	Not linear (variable cannot be in the denominator)

Graphing an equation means finding two or more ordered pairs that satisfy the equation and then plotting those points on the coordinate plane.

Example
Graph $-3x + y = 1$.

Solution
First solve the equation for y.
$$y = 3x + 1$$

Substitute two or more values for x.
If $x = 0$, then $y = 3 \bullet 0 + 1$
$$= 0 + 1$$
$$= 1$$

and $(0, 1)$ is a solution of the equation.
If $x = 1$ then $y = 3 \bullet 1 + 1$
$$= 3 + 1$$
$$= 4$$

and $(1, 4)$ is a solution of the equation.

Just two ordered pairs are necessary to obtain the graph, but a third should be obtained as a check.

If $x = 2$ then $y = 3 \bullet 2 + 1$
$$= 6 + 1$$
$$= 7$$
and $(2, 7)$ is a solution.

To draw the graph of $y = 3x + 1$, simply plot the three ordered pairs $(0, 1)$, $(1, 4)$, and $(2, 7)$ and draw a line through all the points.

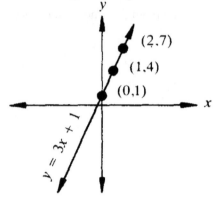

There are two special cases.

Example
Graph $x = -2$.

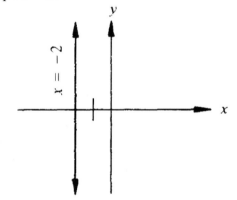

Solution
If x is the only variable in the equation, it is a vertical line, and in this case, it will be two units to the left of the y-axis.

110

Example
Graph $y = 1$.

Solution
If y is the only variable in the equation, it is a horizontal line one unit above the x-axis.

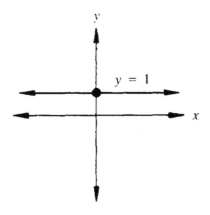

Equations of Circles

A quadratic equation with two unknown letters, both of the second degree and both letters having the same coefficients and like signs, is a circle.

$$x^2 + y^2 = r^2$$

    x and y are both squared and on the same side of the equation.
    x and y have the same coefficients of 1.
    x and y have the same sign, positive.

The center of the circle is the origin $(0, 0)$. The radius of the circle is r.
$$(x - h)^2 + (y - k)^2 = r^2$$
The center of the circle is (h, k). The radius is r.

Example
$x^2 + y^2 = 16$
center at $(0, 0)$
radius = $\sqrt{16}$ = 4

Example
$(x - 4)^2 + (y - 3)^2 = 49$
center at $(4, 3)$
radius = $\sqrt{49}$ = 7

Example
$(x + 2)^2 + (y - 1)^2 = 100$
center at $(-2, 1)$
radius = $\sqrt{100}$ = 10

Example
$$2x^2 + 2y^2 = 18$$
(Divide by 2)
$$x^2 + y^2 = 9$$
center at $(0, 0)$
radius = $\sqrt{9}$ = 3

Example
$x^2 + y^2 = 10$
center at $(0, 0)$
radius = $\sqrt{10}$

Example
$x^2 - 2x + y^2 + 2y = 102$

Solution
Complete the square.
$x^2 - 2x + y^2 + 2y = 98$
$x^2 - 2x + 1 + y^2 + 2y + 1 = 98 + 1 + 1$
$(x - 1)^2 + (y + 1)^2 = 100$
center at $(1, -1)$
radius = $\sqrt{100}$ = 10

Graphing the Conic Sections

A quadratic, or second degree function, is one in which at most the square of a variable, or the product of two variables, or both appear.

The standard form of a quadratic is
$ax^2 + bxy + cy^2 + dx + ey + f = 0$
in which a, b, c, d, e, f are constants and x and y are variables.

The graph of a quadratic function is called a conic section and can be obtained by a plane intersecting a cone of two nappes.

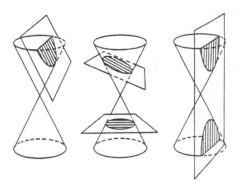

Listed below are the characteristics for identifying these curves.

PARABOLA $y = ax^2 + bx + c$	Only one variable is squared, either x or y. If a is positive, the parabola is open upward. If a is negative, the parabola is open downward. If the y term is squared, the parabola goes right or left.
CIRCLE $x^2 + y^2 = r^2$ center $(0, 0)$ $(x - h)^2 + (y - k)^2 = r^2$ center (h, k)	The variables x and y are both squared and have like signs and like coefficients.
ELLIPSE $\dfrac{x^2}{a^2} + \dfrac{y^2}{b^2} = 1$ center $(0, 0)$ x-intercepts a, $-a$ y-intercepts b, $-b$	The variables x and y are both squared, have like signs but will have unlike coefficients.
HYPERBOLA $\dfrac{x^2}{a^2} - \dfrac{y^2}{b^2} = 1$ equations of asymptotes $y = \dfrac{bx}{a}, y = -\dfrac{bx}{a}$	The variables x and y are both squared and have unlike signs.
HYPERBOLA $xy = k$ where $k \neq 0$ Has the coordinate axes as asymptotes.	This is a special case.

Identify and graph each of the following.

Example

$y = x^2$
Parabola

x	0	±1	±2
y	0	1	4

$y = x^2 + 2$
Parabola

x	0	±1	±2
y	2	3	6

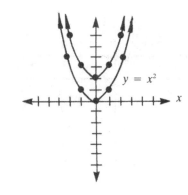

Example
$y = x^2 + 8x + 16$
Parabola

x	-5	-4	-3	-2	-1	0
y	1	0	1	4	9	16

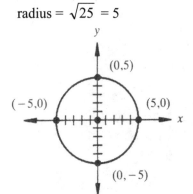

Example
$x^2 + y^2 = 25$
Circle   center at $(0, 0)$
radius $= \sqrt{25} = 5$

112

Example

$(x-2)^2 + (y-1)^2 = 36$

Circle   center at (2, 1)

         radius = $\sqrt{36}$ = 6

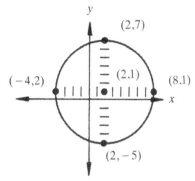

Example

$\dfrac{x^2}{36} + \dfrac{y^2}{4} = 1$

Ellipse   center at (0, 0)

         x-intercept -6, 6

         y-intercept -2, 2

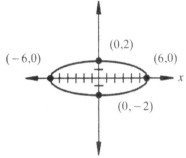

Example

$\dfrac{x^2}{4} + \dfrac{y^2}{9} = 1$

hyperbola

Equations of asymptotes $y = \pm \dfrac{3x}{2}$ (dotted lines)

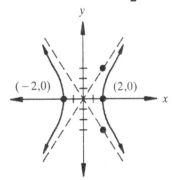

Let the negative variable equal zero and

$$\frac{x^2}{4} = 1$$

$$x^2 = 4$$

$$x = \pm 2$$

The hyperbola crosses the *x*-axis at ±2 and approaches the asymptotes.

Example

$xy = 6$

Hyperbola   The *x* and *y* axes act as
(special case)   asymptotes, and in the
                product *xy*, *x* and *y* are
                either both positive or
                both negative.

-3	-2	-1	0	1	2	3
-2	-3	-6	und	6	3	2

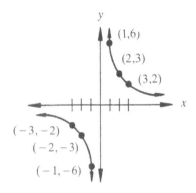

Graphical Solutions to Systems of Equations and/or Inequalities

There are three possible relationships that may exist between two straight lines.

- The two lines may intersect at one and only one point.
- The two lines may intersect at many number of points; in other words, the two lines coincide.
- The two lines may not intersect at all; they will be parallel.

To find the solution to a pair of equations, graph both equations and find the point at which their lines meet.

113

Example

Solve the pair of equations

$x + y = 4$
$-x + y = 2$

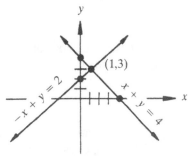

Graph each equation by the slope-intercept method.

$x + y = 4$ $-x + y = 2$

$\quad y = -x + 4$ $\quad y = x + 2$

$\quad m = -\dfrac{1}{1}$ $\quad m = \dfrac{1}{1}$

$\quad b = 4$ $\quad b = 2$

The lines meet at the point (1, 3), which is the solution to both equations. (Check numbers in the equations.

To find the solution to a pair of inequalities, graph them both and find their overlapping regions.

Example

Graph the solution set of the following system.

$x + y \geq 4$
$-x + y \leq 2$

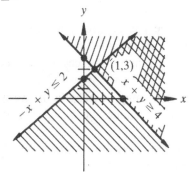

$x + y \geq 4$ $-x + y \leq 2$

$\quad y \geq -x + 4$ $\quad y \leq -x + 2$

$\quad m = -\dfrac{1}{1}$ $\quad m = \dfrac{1}{1}$

$\quad b = 4$ $\quad b = 2$

The graph is the line and all points *above* the line.   The graph is the line and all points *below* the line.

The solution to the system is the cross-hatched region.

To find the solution of a linear equation and a quadratic equation or two quadratics, there may be a number of intersections. Here are some possibilities.

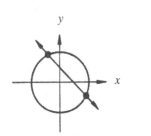

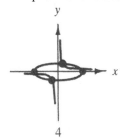

Two points of intersection

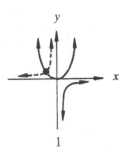

3

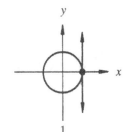

4

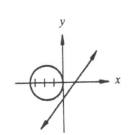

1

1

No points of intersection

114

Orientation Exercises

1. Which ordered pair represents a point that lies on the given graph?

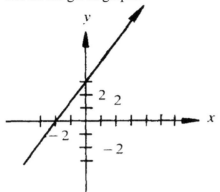

   A. (3, 0)
   B. (1, 2)
   C. (2, 6)
   D. (-1, 1)
   E. (-2, 6)

2. The lines $y = 3$ and $x = 6$ intersect at what point?

   A. (3, 6)
   B. (6, 3)
   C. (0, 0)
   D. (3, 0)
   E. (0, 3)

3. Which of the following is the radius of a circle whose equation is $x^2 + y^2 = 100$?

   A. 1
   B. 10
   C. 20
   D. 50
   E. 100

4. Which of the following is the radius of a circle whose equation is $x^2 + y^2 = 5$?

   A. -25
   B. -5
   C. $\sqrt{5}$
   D. 5
   E. 25

5. Identify the graph of the quadratic equation $y^2 - 4x^2 = 16$.

   A. Parabola
   B. Hyperbola
   C. Circle
   D. Ellipse
   E. Two intersecting lines

6. Identify the graph of the quadratic equation $y^2 + x^2 = 36$.

   A. Parabola
   B. Hyperbola
   C. Circle
   D. Ellipse
   E. Line

7. The graphs of $x^2 + y^2 = 36$ and $xy = 4$ have:

   A. no intersections
   B. two intersections
   C. three intersections
   D. four intersections
   E. more than four intersections

8. How many solutions does the quadratic system $x^2 + y^2 = 25$ and $x^2 + (y - 1)^2 = 4$ have?

   A. 1
   B. 2
   C. 3
   D. 4
   E. None

Practice Exercises

1. An equation of the y-axis is:

   A. $x = 0$
   B. $y = 0$
   C. $x + y = 0$
   D. $x - y = 0$
   E. The y-axis has no equation.

2. What are the (x, y) coordinates of the point at which the line determined by the equation $3x + 2y = 12$ crosses the x-axis?

   A. $(6, 0)$
   B. $(0, 6)$
   C. $(3, 2)$
   D. $(4, 0)$
   E. $(0, 4)$

3. Which of the following is the center of a circle whose equation is $x^2 - 2x + y^2 + 2y = 102$?

   A. $(-2, 2)$
   B. $(2, -2)$
   C. $(0, 0)$
   D. $(1, 1)$
   E. $(1, -1)$

4. Which of the following is the radius of a circle whose equation is $2x^2 + 2y^2 = 128$?

   A. 8
   B. 16
   C. 32
   D. 64
   E. 128

5. Which of the following is the graph of $y = x^2 - 6x + 9$?

   A.
   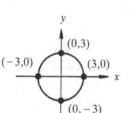

   D.
   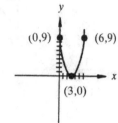

   B.
   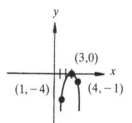

   E.
   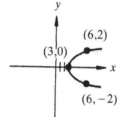

   C.
   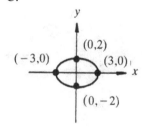

6. The graph of $xy = 10$ is:

   A. a circle
   B. a hyperbola
   C. a parabola
   D. an ellipse
   E. a straight line

7. The graph of $4x^2 - 9y^2 = 36$ is:

   A. a circle
   B. a hyperbola
   C. a parabola
   D. an ellipse
   E. a straight line

8. The shaded region in the figure represents the solution set of:

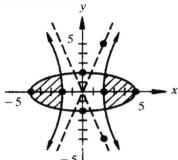

A.
$$\frac{x^2}{25} + \frac{y^2}{4} \leq 1$$

$$\frac{x^2}{25} - \frac{y^2}{4} \leq 1$$

B.
$$\frac{x^2}{4} + \frac{y^2}{25} \leq 1$$

$$\frac{x^2}{4} - \frac{y^2}{25} \leq 1$$

C.
$$\frac{x^2}{25} + \frac{y^2}{4} \leq 1$$

$$\frac{x^2}{4} - \frac{y^2}{25} \geq 1$$

D.
$$\frac{x^2}{25} + \frac{y^2}{4} \leq 1$$

$$\frac{x^2}{4} - \frac{y^2}{25} \leq 1$$

E.
$$\frac{x^2}{4} + \frac{y^2}{25} \leq 1$$

$$\frac{x^2}{25} - \frac{y^2}{4} \geq 1$$

9. If $xy = 12$ (hyperbola) and $x^2 + y^2 = 25$ (circle), a pair of values of x and y may be:

A. (2, 6)
B. (4, 5)
C. (3, -4)
D. (-3, -4)
E. (-3, 4)

Practice Test

1. Which of the following equations is linear?

    A. $x^2 + y^2 = 16$
    B. $y = x^2 + 16$
    C. $x + y = 16$
    D. $xy = 16$
    E. $x + \dfrac{1}{y} = 16$

2. The equation whose graph is shown below is:

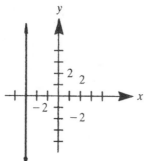

    A. $x + y = -3$
    B. $x - y = -3$
    C. $y = -3$
    D. $x = -3$
    E. The graph has no equation.

3. What is the equation of the circle graphed below?

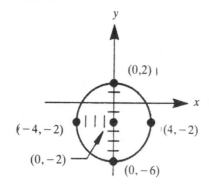

    A. $x^2 + (y - 2)^2 = 8$
    B. $x^2 + (y - 2)^2 = 16$
    C. $x^2 + (y + 2)^2 = 8$
    D. $x^2 + (y + 2)^2 = 16$
    E. $x^2 + y^2 = 16$

4. Which type of conic is described by the equation $3x^2 + 3y^2 - 12x + 12y + 18 = 0$?

    A. Circle
    B. Ellipse
    C. Parabola
    D. Hyperbola
    E. Two intersecting straight lines

5. What is the equation of the ellipse graphed below?

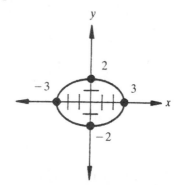

    A. $\dfrac{y^2}{4} - \dfrac{x^2}{9} = 1$

    B. $\dfrac{x^2}{6} - \dfrac{y^2}{4} = 1$

    C. $\dfrac{x^2}{9} - \dfrac{y^2}{4} = 1$

    D. $\dfrac{x^2}{9} + \dfrac{y^2}{4} = 1$

    E. $\dfrac{x^2}{6} + \dfrac{y^2}{4} = 1$

6. Which graph shows the equation $y = -x^2$?

A.

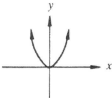

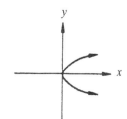

B.

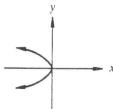

C.

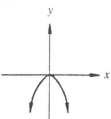

D.

E.

7. Which of the following equations could represent the graph?

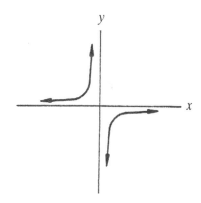

A. $x + y = 12$
B. $xy = 16$
C. $x - y = 8$
D. $xy = -4$
E. $x - 2y = 6$

8. The intersection of graphs of
$$\frac{x^2}{a^2} + \frac{y^2}{b^2} = 1 \text{ when } a \neq 0, b \neq 0, \text{ and } y = mx + b,$$
consists of how many points?

A. At least one
B. At most two
C. Exactly two
D. At most four
E. Never exactly one

9. The graphs of $x^2 + y^2 = 25$ and $xy = -4$ have:

A. no intersections
B. two intersections
C. three intersections
D. four intersections
E. more than four intersections

Lines, Segments, and Rays

The following examples should help you distinguish between lines, segments, and rays. The three undefined terms in geometry are **point**, **line**, and **plane**.

• X   represents point X—It has no size.

represents line *YZ*—It extends without end in both directions.

represents plane *W*—It has a flat surface that extends indefinitely in all directions.

Segment = A part of a line consisting of two endpoints and all the points between them.

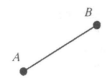

Segment $\overline{AB}$ or segment $\overline{BA}$

Ray = A part of a line consisting of one endpoint and extending without end in the other direction.

Ray *CD* (endpoint must be named first) or $\overrightarrow{CD}$

Collinear points are points that lie on the same line.

Non-collinear points are points that do not all lie on the same line.

NOTE:

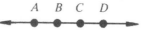

$\overline{AD}$ and $\overline{DA}$ are the same segment.

But $\overrightarrow{AD}$ and $\overrightarrow{DA}$ are different rays (different endpoints).

$\overleftrightarrow{AD}$ and $\overleftrightarrow{DA}$ are the same line.

$\overrightarrow{BA}$ and $\overrightarrow{BC}$ are opposite rays (same endpoints).

Measurement and Construction of Right, Acute, and Obtuse Angles

Naming Angles

An angle is formed by two rays having a common endpoint. This endpoint is called the **vertex** of the angle. Angles are measured in degrees.

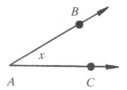

Angles may be named in three different ways:
(1) by the letter at its vertex ($\angle A$).
(2) by three capital letters with the vertex letter in the center ($\angle BAC$ or $\angle CAB$).
(3) by a lower case letter or a number placed inside the angle ($\angle x$).

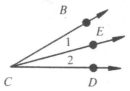

NOTE: Angle *C* cannot be the name for the angle because there are three angles that have the common vertex, *C*. They are angles *BCE*, *ECD*, and *BCD*. Angle *BCE* may also be named $\angle ECB$ or $\angle 1$. Angles 1 and 2 are adjacent angles since they share a common vertex, C, and a common side, CE, between them.

Classifying Angles

Angles are classified according to the number of degrees contained in the angle.

Type of Angle	Number of Degrees
acute angle	less than 90°
right angle	90°
obtuse angle	greater than 90° but less than 180°
straight angle	180°

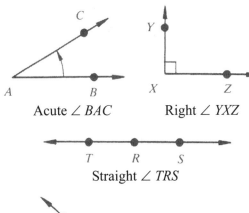

Acute ∠ BAC   Right ∠ YXZ

Straight ∠ TRS

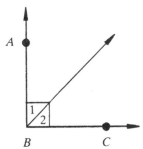

Obtuse ∠ EDF

Complementary and Supplementary Angles

Complementary angles are two angles whose sum is 90°.

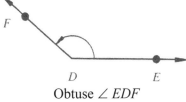

Since ∠ABC measures 90°, angles 1 and 2 are complementary angles.

Supplementary angles are two angles whose sum is 180°.

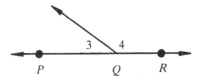

Since ∠ PQR = 180°, angles 3 and 4 are supplementary angles. This is also an example of a linear pair, adjacent angles such that two of the rays are opposite rays that form a linear pair.

Example
If $LN \perp NM$, express the number of degrees in x in terms of y.

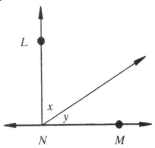

Solution
Since $LN \perp MN$, ∠ LNM measures 90°.

$$x + y = 90°$$
$$\underline{-y-y} \text{ (using the additive inverse)}$$
$$x = 90° - y$$

Example
If PQ is a straight line, express y in terms of x.

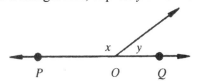

Solution
A straight line forms a straight angle. Therefore

y in terms of x
$$x + y = 180°$$
$$\underline{-x-x} \text{ (using the additive inverse)}$$
$$y = 180° - x$$

x in terms of y
$$x + y = 180°$$
$$\underline{-y-y} \text{ (using the additive inverse)}$$
$$x = 180° - y$$

121

Example

If $BA \perp AC$, find the number of degrees in angle x.

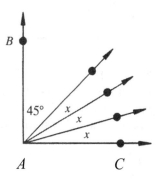

Solution

Since $BA \perp AC$, $\angle BAC = 90°$. Therefore,

$x° + x° + x° + 45° = 90°$

$3x° + 45° = 90°$ (combining like terms)

$\underline{ -45° -45°}$ (using the additive inverse)

$3x° = 45°$ (using the multiplicative inverse)

$$\frac{1}{3}(3x°) = (45°)\frac{1}{3}$$

$x° = 15°$

Example

Find the number of degrees in angle x.

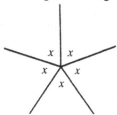

Solution

Since the five angles center about a point, their sum is $360°$. Therefore,

$x + x + x + x + x = 360°$ (combining like terms)

$5x = 360°$

$$\frac{1}{5}(5x) = (360°)\frac{1}{5}$$ (using the multiplicative inverse)

$x = 72°$

Vertical Angles

Vertical angles are the non-adjacent angles formed when two straight lines intersect.

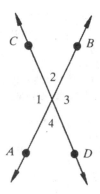

Angles 1 and 3 are vertical angles. Angles 2 and 4 are also vertical angles. If $m \angle 2 = 50°$, then $m \angle 1 + m \angle 2 = 180°$ (straight $\angle AB$) and $\angle 1$ measures $130°$. Also, $m \angle 1 + m \angle 2 = 180°$ (straight $\angle CD$), and $\angle 3$ measures $130°$. Since supplements of the same angle are equal, vertical angles contain the same number of degrees. Thus, $\angle 1 \cong \angle 3$ and $\angle 2 \cong \angle 4$.

Example

Find x, y, and z.

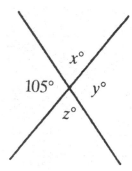

Solution

Since vertical angles are equal, $\angle y = 105°$. The same is true for x and z: $x = z$. Any two adjacent angles such as z and $105°$ are supplementary. Therefore,

$z + 105 = 180$

$\underline{ -105 -105}$ (using the additive inverse)

$z = 75°$

$x = 75°$

and $y = 105°$

Perpendicular Lines

Perpendicular lines are lines that meet and form right angles. The symbol for perpendicular is $\perp$.

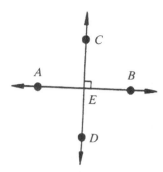

$\overrightarrow{AB}$ is perpendicular to $\overline{CD}$

or

$\overrightarrow{AB} \perp \overline{CD}$

If two intersecting lines form adjacent angles whose measures are equal, the lines are perpendicular.

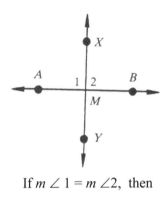

If $m \angle 1 = m \angle 2$, then

$\overrightarrow{AB} \perp \overline{XY}$

Perpendicular lines form four right angles.

Parallel Lines and Transversals

Angles Formed by Parallel Lines

The figure illustrates two parallel lines, *AB* and *CD*, and an intersecting line *EF*, called the **transversal**.

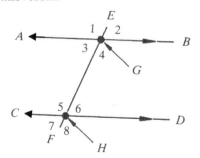

The arrows in the diagram indicate that the lines are parallel. The symbol ‖ means "is parallel to": $\overline{AB} \parallel \overline{CD}$.

There are relationships between pairs of angles with which you are familiar from your previous studies. Angles 1 and 4 are vertical angles and congruent. Angles 5 and 7 are supplementary angles, and their measures add up to 180°.

Corresponding angles are two angles that lie in corresponding positions in relation to the parallel lines and the transversal. For example, $\angle 1$ and $\angle 5$ are corresponding angles. So are $\angle 4$ and $\angle 8$. Other pairs of corresponding angles are $\angle 2$ and $\angle 6$, $\angle 3$ and $\angle 7$.

Angles 3 and 5 are interior angles on the same side of the transversal. These angles are supplementary. Angles 4 and 6 are also supplementary.

Alternate interior angles are two angles that lie on opposite (alternate) sides of the transversal and between the parallel lines. For example, $\angle 3$ and $\angle 6$ are alternate interior angles, as are $\angle 4$ and $\angle 5$.

If two lines are parallel, corresponding angles are congruent or equal, and alternate interior angles are congruent or equal.

In the diagram below, if $l \parallel m$, the alternate interior angles are congruent, and $\angle x \cong \angle z$. Since corresponding angles are congruent, $\angle y \cong \angle z$. Therefore, $\angle x \cong \angle y \cong \angle z$.

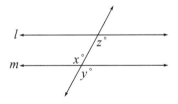

123

Example

$l \parallel m$ and $m \angle A = 100°$. Find the number of degrees in angles b, c, d, e, f, g, and h.

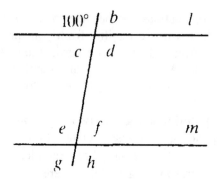

Example

$AB \parallel ED$, $\angle B = 70°$ and $\angle ACB = 65°$. Find the number of degrees in x.

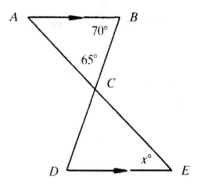

Solution

Because $\angle A$ and $\angle d$ are vertical angles, $\angle d$ measures 100°. Using supplementary angles, $m \angle b = 180° - 100° = 80°$ and $m \angle c = 180° - 100° = 80°$; therefore $m \angle b = m\angle c = 80°$. Use either property of parallel lines—corresponding angles or alternate interior angles—to obtain the remainder of the answers. For example, $m \angle b = m \angle f$ by corresponding angles or $m \angle c = m \angle f$ by alternate interior angles. Thus: $m \angle b = m \angle c = m \angle g = m \angle f = 80°$ and $m \angle e = m \angle h = m \angle d = 100°$.

Solution

Knowing two angles of $\triangle ABC$, $\angle A = 45°$. Angles A and E are alternate interior angles. Therefore, $\angle A = \angle E$, since $AB \parallel DE$. Thus $\angle x = 45°$.

124

Orientation Exercises

1. Which rays form the sides of ∠*ABC*?

    A. $\overrightarrow{AB}$, $\overrightarrow{AC}$ D. $\overrightarrow{BA}$, $\overrightarrow{BC}$
    B. $\overrightarrow{AB}$, $\overrightarrow{CB}$ E. None of the above
    C. $\overrightarrow{AC}$, $\overrightarrow{BD}$

2. In the figure below, line *a* is:

    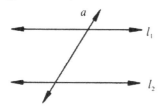

    A. a bisector
    B. parallel
    C. a transversal
    D. perpendicular
    E. an altitude

3. Which angles appear to be obtuse?

    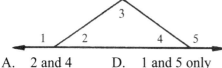

    A. 2 and 4   D. 1 and 5 only
    B. 2, 3, and 4 E. 3 only
    C. 1, 3, and 5

4. Which angles form a pair of vertical angles?

    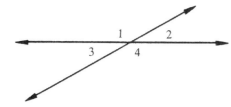

    A. 1 and 2   D. 4 and 1
    B. 2 and 4   E. 1 and 3
    C. 3 and 4

5. At how many points will two lines that are perpendicular intersect?
    A. 0   D. 3
    B. 1   E. 4
    C. 2

6. If two intersecting lines form congruent adjacent angles, the lines are:

    A. parallel
    B. oblique
    C. horizontal
    D. vertical
    E. perpendicular

7. In the figure below, parallel lines $\overleftrightarrow{AC}$ and $\overleftrightarrow{BD}$ intersect transversal $\overleftrightarrow{MN}$ at points *x* and *y*. ∠ *MXA* and ∠ *MYB* are known as:

    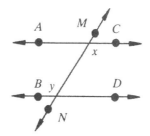

    A. vertical angles
    B. alternate interior angles
    C. complementary angles
    D. supplementary angles
    E. corresponding angles

8. In the figure below, $\overleftrightarrow{AB} \parallel \overleftrightarrow{CD}$ and $\overleftrightarrow{RS}$ and $\overleftrightarrow{PQ}$ are straight lines. Which of the following is true?

    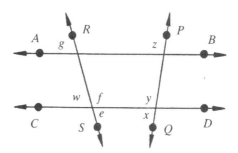

    A. $g = z$ D. $g = x$
    B. $g = y$ E. $g = e$
    C. $g = f$

Practice Exercises

1. Three points, R, S, and T are collinear. Point S lies between R and T. If $RS = \dfrac{2}{3} RT$ and $RS = 48$, find $\dfrac{1}{2} RT$.

   A. 72   D. 36
   B. 60   E. 24
   C. 48

2. Points E, F, and G are collinear. If $EF = 8$ and $EG = 12$, which point cannot lie between the other two?

   A. E D. F and G
   B. F E. Cannot be determined
   C. G

3. If PRQ is a straight line, find the number of degrees in $\angle w$.

   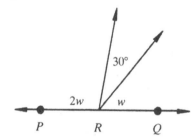

   A. 30   D. 70
   B. 50   E. 100
   C. 60

4. In the figure, if $\overrightarrow{AB}$ is a straight line and $m\angle CDB = 60°$, what is the measure of $\angle CDA$?

   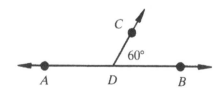

   A. 15°   D. 90°
   B. 30°   E. 120°
   C. 60°

5. Line XY is perpendicular to line CD at D. Which conclusion can be drawn?
   A. $XD = DY$
   B. $XY = CD$
   C. $m\angle XDC = 90°$
   D. $m\angle XDC = 90°$ and $XD = DY$
   E. All of the above

6. In the figure, a, b, and c are lines with $a \perp b$. Which angles are congruent?

   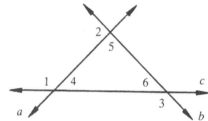

   A. $\angle 4, \angle 5$ D. $\angle 2, \angle 5$
   B. $\angle 4, \angle 6$ E. $\angle 2, \angle 6$
   C. $\angle 4, \angle 3$

7. $l \parallel m$, and $AB = AC$. Find x.

   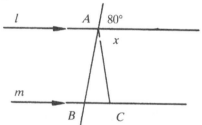

   A. 40   D. 100
   B. 60   E. None of the above
   C. 80

8. In the figure, if lines r and s are parallel, what is the value of x?

   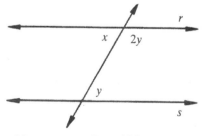

   A. 30   D. 120
   B. 60   E. 150
   C. 90

126

Practice Test

1. In the figure, *U*, *V*, *W*, and *X* are collinear. $\overline{UX}$ is 50 units long, $\overline{UW}$ is 22 units long, and $\overline{VX}$ is 29 units long. How many units long is $\overline{VW}$?

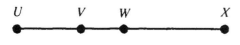

   A. 1
   B. 7
   C. $7\frac{1}{2}$
   D. 21
   E. 28

2. How many different rays can be named by three different collinear points?
   A. 0
   B. 1
   C. 2
   D. 3
   E. 4

3. A 60° angle is bisected, and each of the resulting angles is trisected. Which of the following could *not* be the degree measure of an angle formed by any two of the rays?
   A. 10
   B. 20
   C. 25
   D. 40
   E. 50

4. Solve for *x*.

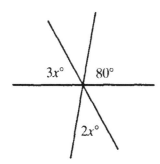

   A. 45
   B. 40
   C. 20
   D. 16
   E. None of the above

5. *P*, *Q*, *R*, *S*, and *T* are five distinct lines in a plane. If $P \perp Q$, $Q \perp R$, $S \perp T$, and $R \parallel S$, all of the following are true, except:

   A. $P \parallel R$
   B. $P \parallel S$
   C. $P \perp T$
   D. $S \perp Q$
   E. $Q \perp T$

6. In the figure, if $l_1 \parallel l_2$, $l_2 \parallel l_3$, and $l_1 \perp l_4$, which of the following statements must be true?

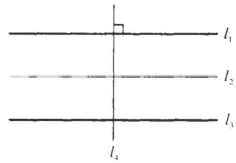

   I. $l_1 \parallel l_3$
   II. $l_2 \perp l_4$
   III. $l_3 \perp l_4$

   A. None
   B. I only
   C. I and II only
   D. II and III only
   E. I, II, and III

7. When two parallel lines are cut by a transversal, how many pairs of corresponding angles are formed?

   A. 1
   B. 2
   C. 3
   D. 4
   E. 8

8. If $a \parallel b \parallel c$ and $c \perp d$, which of the following statements is true?

   A. $a \parallel d$
   B. $a \perp c$
   C. $b \parallel d$
   D. $b \perp c$
   E. $a \perp d$

127

Properties of Triangles

Classification by Sides

Triangles that are classified according to the lengths of their sides are equilateral, isosceles, or scalene.

Scalene Triangle: A triangle with no congruent sides.

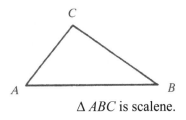

$\triangle ABC$ is scalene.

Isosceles Triangle: A triangle with two or more congruent sides.

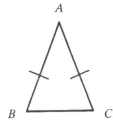

$\overline{AB} \cong \overline{AC}$, $\overline{BC}$ is called the base.

Angle A is the vertex angle,
$\angle B$ and $\angle C$ are the base angles.
$\angle B \cong \angle C$.

Equilateral Triangle: A triangle with three congruent sides.

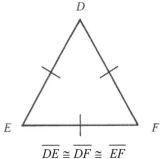

$\overline{DE} \cong \overline{DF} \cong \overline{EF}$
Each angle is congruent to the other angles.
$\angle D \cong \angle E \cong \angle F$.
Each has a degree measure of 60°.

Classification by Angles

Triangles can be classified by their angles. An **acute triangle** is a triangle that has three **acute angles**. An acute angle is an angle whose measure is less than 90°.

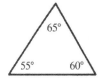
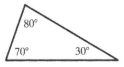

An **obtuse angle** is an angle whose degree measure is greater than 90° but less than 180°. An **obtuse triangle** has one obtuse angle.

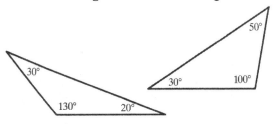

A **right triangle** is a triangle that has one right angle. A right angle is an angle whose degree measure is 90°. The symbol for a right angle in a triangle is shown below.

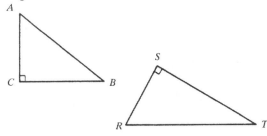

NOTE: In a right triangle, the sides have special names. The side opposite the 90° angle is the hypotenuse (the longest side of the right triangle). The two sides that form the 90° angle are called legs.

Thus, $\overline{AC}$ and $\overline{CB}$, $\overline{RS}$ and $\overline{ST}$ are legs. $\overline{AB}$ and $\overline{RT}$ are each called a hypotenuse.

Example

Classify each triangle pictured by the angles shown.

(A)

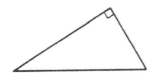

(B)

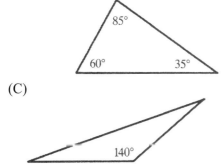

(C)

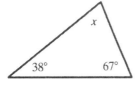

(A) The triangle has a right angle; therefore, it is a right triangle.
(B) The triangle is acute since each angle is acute.
(C) The obtuse angle identifies an obtuse triangle.

Sum of the Angles

The sum of the measure of the angles of any triangle is 180°.

Example
Find x.

Solution
$x + 38 + 67 = 180$
$\quad x + 105 = 180$ (combining similar terms)
$\quad \underline{\quad -105 \quad -105\quad}$ (using the additive inverse)
$\qquad\quad x = 75$

Example
An isosceles triangle has a vertex angle whose degree measure is 48°. Find the degree measure of each base angle.

Solution

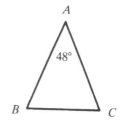

$\overline{AB} \cong \overline{AC}$ and vertex $m\angle A = 48°$.
Thus: $48° + m\angle B + m\angle C = 180°$

Let x represent the number of degrees in angles B and C

(by substitution)	$48 + x + x = 180$
(combining similar terms)	$2x + 48 = 180$
(using the additive inverse)	$\underline{\quad -48 \quad -48\quad}$
	$2x = 132$
(using the multiplicative inverse)	$\frac{1}{2}(2x) = (132)\frac{1}{2}$
	$x = 66$

Therefore, $\angle B$ measures 66 and $\angle C$ measures 66°.

Perimeter of Triangles

The perimeter of a triangle is the sum of the lengths of its sides.

Example
Find the perimeter of $\triangle ABC$.

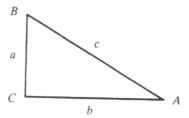

Solution
Perimeter = $a + b + c$

A **median** of a triangle is a segment from one vertex to the midpoint of the opposite side.

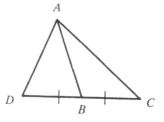

An **altitude** of a triangle is a segment from one vertex perpendicular to the opposite side.

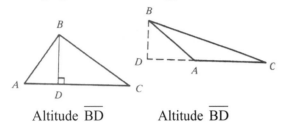

Altitude $\overline{BD}$ Altitude $\overline{BD}$

In $\triangle XYZ$, $\angle 1$ is an exterior angle of the triangle because it forms a linear pair with an angle of the triangle.

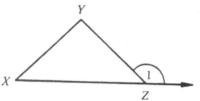

Angles X and Y are called remote interior angles of the triangle with respect to $\angle 1$.

NOTE: $m\angle 1 = m\angle X + m\angle Y$.

Identification of Plane Geometric Figures

A polygon is a plane figure consisting of a certain number of sides. If the sides are equal, the figure is referred to as **regular**.

    A triangle has 3 sides.
    A quadrilateral has 4 sides.
    A pentagon has 5 sides.
    A hexagon has 6 sides.
    A heptagon has 7 sides
    An octagon has 8 sides.
    A nonagon has 9 sides.
    A decagon has 10 sides
    A dodecagon has 12 sides.
    An n-gon has n sides.

Angles of a Polygon

The sum of the measures of the angles of a triangle is 180°. The sum of the measures of the angles of a quadrilateral is 360°. The sum of the measures of the *interior* angles of a polygon is
$$S = 180(n - 2)$$
where n equals the number of sides.

An exterior angle of a polygon is an angle that forms a linear pair with one of the interior angles of the polygon.

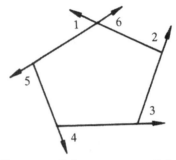

NOTE: The sum of the measures of the exterior angles of any polygon is 360°.

Remember, triangles (polygons of three sides) are classified as:
    Acute—All three angles are acute angles
    Obtuse—Contains one obtuse angle
    Right—Contains one right angle
    Equiangular—All three angles are equal
    Scalene—No two sides equal
    Isosceles—Two equal sides
    Equilateral—All sides are equal

Quadrilaterals (polygons of four sides) are very important in geometry.

A parallelogram is a quadrilateral whose opposite sides are parallel.

A rectangle is a quadrilateral whose angles are right angles; it is a special kind of parallelogram.

A rhombus is a parallelogram with adjacent sides congruent.

A square is a four-sided figure with four right angles and four equal sides; it is a parallelogram.

A trapezoid is a quadrilateral with exactly one pair of parallel sides.

An isosceles trapezoid is a trapezoid whose non-parallel sides are congruent.

Congruent and Similar Triangles

A correspondence between two triangles is a congruence if the corresponding angles and the corresponding sides are congruent. Triangles that have the same *shape* and *size* are congruent.

If $\angle A \cong \angle X$ $\overline{AB} \cong \overline{XY}$

     $\angle B \cong \angle Y$ $\overline{BC} \cong \overline{YZ}$

     $\angle C \cong \angle Z$ $\overline{AC} \cong \overline{XZ}$

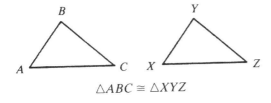

$$\triangle ABC \cong \triangle XYZ$$

There are other ways to show triangles are congruent.
(A = Angle; S = Side)

SAS Postulate (Side-included angle-side)

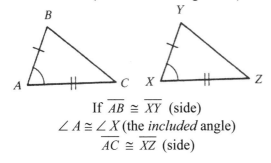

If $\overline{AB} \cong \overline{XY}$ (side)

$\angle A \cong \angle X$ (the *included* angle)

$\overline{AC} \cong \overline{XZ}$ (side)

ASA Postulate (Angle-included side-angle)

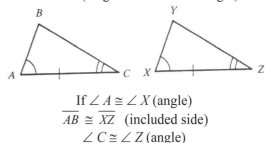

If $\angle A \cong \angle X$ (angle)

$\overline{AB} \cong \overline{XZ}$ (included side)

$\angle C \cong \angle Z$ (angle)

SSS Postulate (side-side-side)

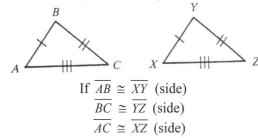

If $\overline{AB} \cong \overline{XY}$ (side)

$\overline{BC} \cong \overline{YZ}$ (side)

$\overline{AC} \cong \overline{XZ}$ (side)

If they are right triangles:

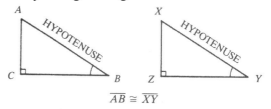

$$\overline{AB} \cong \overline{XY}$$

HA Postulate:
(hypotenuse-acute angle)   If $\angle B \cong \angle Y$

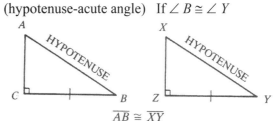

$$\overline{AB} \cong \overline{XY}$$

HL Postulate
(hypotenuse-leg)   If $\overline{CB} \cong \overline{ZY}$

Also, if two triangles have a side and two angles of one congruent to a side and two angles of the other, then the triangles are congruent (SAA).

Two triangles are similar if the corresponding angles are *congruent*. AAA similarity theorem
or
AA similarity theorem

Other theorems used to show triangles similar are

SAS similarity theorem
SSS similarity theorem

where the angles are congruent and the sides proportional.

NOTE: In addition, the perimeters, altitudes, and medians of similar triangles are proportional to any pair of corresponding sides.

The following diagrams are examples of similar triangles.

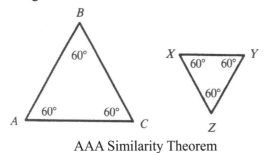

AAA Similarity Theorem

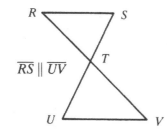

$\overline{DE} \parallel \overline{AC}$

$\angle A \cong \angle BDE$
$\angle C \cong \angle BCA$
AA Similarity Theorem

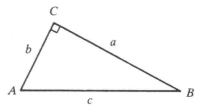

$\overline{RS} \parallel \overline{UV}$

$\angle R \cong \angle V$ (alternate)
$\angle RTS \cong \angle VTU$ (vertical angles)
AA Similarity Theorem

Pythagorean Theorem

In a right triangle, the side opposite the right angle is called the **hypotenuse**, and the other two sides are called the **legs**.

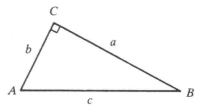

In the figure, $\overline{AB}$ is the hypotenuse whose measure is c. $\overline{AC}$ and $\overline{CB}$ are the legs whose measures are b and a, respectively.

In any right triangle, the square of the measure of the hypotenuse is equal to the sum of the squares of the measures of the legs. Thus: hypotenuse^2 = leg^2 + leg^2, or $c^2 = a^2 + b^2$, represents the Pythagorean Theorem.

This theorem can be used to find the measure of a third side of a right triangle if the measures of the other two sides are known.

Example
If $PQ = 5$ and $PR = 12$, find QR.

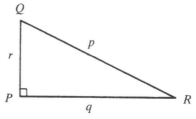

Solution
$p^2 = q^2 + r^2$
$p^2 = 12^2 + 5^2$
$p^2 = 144 + 25$
$p^2 = 169$
$p = \sqrt{169} = 13$

Example
Find X in its reduced form.

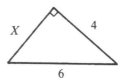

leg^2 + leg^2 = hyp^2 (Pythagorean Theorem)

Solution

$$x^2 + 4^2 = 6^2$$
$$x^2 + 16 = 36$$
$$x^2 = 20$$
$$x = \sqrt{20}$$
$$x = \sqrt{4}\sqrt{5}$$
$$x = 2\sqrt{5}$$

NOTE: There are sets of numbers that satisfy the Pythagorean Theorem. These sets of numbers are called Pythagorean triples.

You should memorize the most common sets of Pythagorean triples

$\{3, 4, 5\}$
$\{6, 8, 10\}$
$\{5, 12, 13\}$ ⟶ for example $5^2 + 12^2 = 13^2$
$\{8, 15, 17\}$ $25 + 144 = 169$
$\{7, 24, 25\}$ $169 = 169$

Ratio of Sides in 30°-60°-90° Triangles and 45°-45°-90° Triangles

There are two special right triangles that deserve your attention. The special properties regarding these triangles can be found by using the Pythagorean Theorem.

30°-60°-90° Triangle: This special triangle is formed by starting with an equilateral triangle and drawing an altitude.

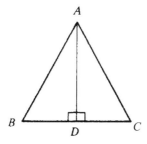

$\triangle ABC$ is equilateral.
$\overline{AD}$ is an altitude.

The altitude drawn to the base of an isosceles triangle bisects the vertex angle and meets the base at the midpoint (or center).

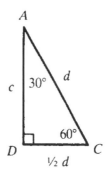

Memorize this:
In a 30°-60°-90° right triangle, *the side opposite the 30° angle* is equal in length to one-half the hypotenuse. *The side opposite the 60° angle* is equal in length to one-half the hypotenuse times $\sqrt{3}$.

Example
$\triangle DEF$ is a 30°-60°-90° triangle, and $\overline{EF} = 4$. Find the measure of $\overline{DF}$ and $\overline{DE}$.

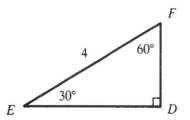

Solution
$\overline{DF}$ is the side opposite the 30° angle, so its measure is one-half the hypotenuse.
Since $\overline{EF} = 4$, $\overline{DF} = 2$.
$\overline{DE}$ is the side opposite the 60° angle, so its measure is one-half the hypotenuse times $\sqrt{3}$.

$$\overline{DE} = \frac{1}{2} \cdot 4 \cdot \sqrt{3} = 2\sqrt{3}.$$

Example
$\triangle PQR$ is a 30°-60°-90° triangle and $PQ = 4$. Find QR and PR.

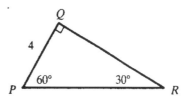

133

Solution

PQ is the side opposite the 30° angle and its measure is one-half the hypotenuse *PR*.

Thus, *PR* = 8.

QR, the side opposite the 60° angle, is one half the hypotenuse times $\sqrt{3}$.

$$QR = \frac{1}{2} \bullet 8 \bullet \sqrt{3} = 4\sqrt{3}$$

45°-45°-90° Triangle: This special right triangle is formed by drawing a diagonal in a square. A diagonal is a line drawn in the polygon that joins any two nonconsecutive vertices.

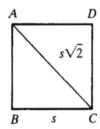

In the figure, $\overline{AC}$ is a diagonal. A diagonal of a square
- divides the square into two congruent isosceles triangles
- bisects two angles of the square
- forms two 45°-45°-90° right triangles.

Memorize this:

In a 45°-45°-90° right isosceles triangle the hypotenuse or the length of the diagonal of the square is found by **multiplying** the length of the side of the square by $\sqrt{2}$.

To find the side of the square or one of the legs of the 45°-45°-90° triangle, *divide* the hypotenuse by $\sqrt{2}$ or take one-half the hypotenuse and multiply by $\sqrt{2}$.

Example

In the figure, *ABC* is a 45°-45°-90° triangle with *AC* = 6. Find *AB* and *BC*.

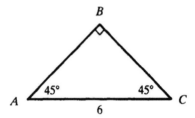

Solution

AB = 6 divided by $\sqrt{2}$

or

$\frac{1}{2} \bullet$ hypotenuse $\bullet \sqrt{2}$

$\frac{1}{2} \bullet 6\sqrt{2} = 3\sqrt{2}$

Since *AB* = *BC*, *BC* = $3\sqrt{2}$

Orientation Exercises

1. In the figure, $\angle P$ measures 30°. $\overline{PS}$ is a line segment and $PQ = QT = TR = RS$. Find the number of degrees in $\angle QTR$.

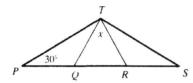

   A. 10°   D. 60°
   B. 20°   E. 80°
   C. 40°

2. In the figure, $AC = CD$. Find the number of degrees in $\angle ADE$.

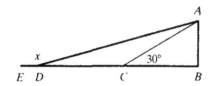

   A. 105°   D. 150°
   B. 120°   E. 165°
   C. 135°

3. A polygon is not a triangle if it has exactly:
   A. three sides
   B. three angles
   C. one of its angles measuring 135°
   D. two perpendicular sides
   E. two parallel sides

4. In quadrilateral $ABCD$, the measures of $\angle A$, $\angle B$, and $\angle C$ are 35°, 160°, and 35°, respectively. What is the measure of $\angle D$?

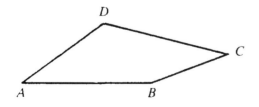

   A. 120°   D. 170°
   B. 130°   E. 230°
   C. 160°

5. If the following information is given, by what authority is $\triangle ABC \cong \triangle EFG$?

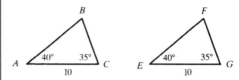

   A. SAS   D. SSA
   B. ASA   E. AAA
   C. SSS

6. In the figure, RST is a triangle and $\overline{XS} \cong \overline{YT}$. Triangles SXT and TSY are:

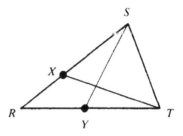

   A. $\cong$ by SSS
   B. $\cong$ by SAS
   C. $\cong$ by ASA
   D. $\sim$ by ASA
   E. Not necessarily $\cong$ or $\sim$.

7. In the figure, ABC is a right angle, $\overline{AB}$ is 4 units long, and $\overline{BC}$ is 6 units long. How many units long is $\overline{AC}$?

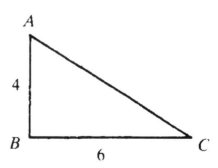

   A. 2   D. $2\sqrt{13}$
   B. $\sqrt{10}$ E. 10
   C. $2\sqrt{5}$

135

8. A right triangle with legs of length 7 inches and 24 inches has a perimeter, in inches, of:

A. 31   D. 168
B. 56   E. None of the above
C. 84

9. If the hypotenuse of a right triangle is 8 inches long and one acute angle measures $60°$, one leg must have a length, in inches, of:

A. $2\dfrac{2}{3}$ D. 6

B. 4   E. $6\sqrt{3}$

C. $4\sqrt{2}$

10. The length of a side of a square is $4\sqrt{2}$. What would be the length of the square's diagonal?

A. 4   D. $8\sqrt{2}$

B. $4\sqrt{2}$ E. 16

C. 8

Practice Exercises

1. In the figure, the three triangles are equilateral and share a common vertex. Find the value of $x + y + z$.

   A. 90°
   B. 120°
   C. 180°
   D. 360°
   E. Cannot be determined from the information given

2. In the figure, $\angle C$ measures 90°, $\overline{CB}$ and $\overline{AD}$ are straight line segments, and $\angle BED$ measures 50°. What is the measure of $\angle A$?

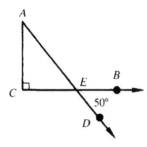

   A. 40°   D. 100°
   B. 50°   E. 130°
   C. 90°

3. If a straight line is drawn from one vertex of a pentagon to another vertex, which of the following pairs of polygons could be produced?

   A. Two triangles
   B. Two quadrilaterals
   C. A triangle and a quadrilateral
   D. A quadrilateral and a pentagon
   E. All of the above

4. How many sides does a decagon have?
   A. 5   D. 10
   B. 6   E. 12
   C. 8

5. In the figure, ΔABC is similar to ΔDEF. What is the length of $\overline{DE}$?

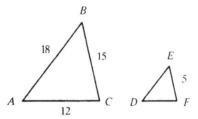

   A. $3\dfrac{1}{3}$ D. $7\dfrac{1}{2}$
   B. $4\dfrac{1}{6}$ E. None of the above
   C. 6

6. In the figure below, E is the midpoint of $\overline{BC}$, and $\overline{RE}$ and $\overline{SB}$ are each perpendicular to $\overline{BC}$. If CE is 20 and SB is 30, how long is the perimeter of quadrilateral $REBS$?

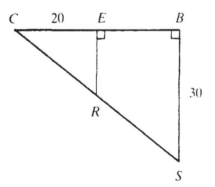

   A. 50   D. 120
   B. 70   E. 220
   C. 90

137

7. In the figure, $\triangle RST$ is a right triangle. Hypotenuse $\overline{RS}$ is 8 units long, and side $\overline{RT}$ is 4 units long. How many units long is side $\overline{TS}$?

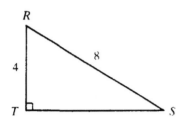

A. $2\sqrt{3}$ D. 8
B. 4   E. None of the above
C. $4\sqrt{3}$

8. In the figure below, what is the length of the segment AB?

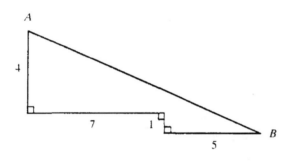

A. 11   D. 16
B. 13   E. 17
C. $5 + \sqrt{66}$

9. In the figure below, $AB = \dfrac{1}{2}AC$ and $\angle ABC$ is a right angle. What is the measure of $\angle ACB$?

A. 25°   D. 45°
B. 30°   E. 60°
C. 40°

10. What is the length of a side of a square with a diagonal of length $5\sqrt{2}$ units?

A. $\dfrac{5\sqrt{2}}{2}$ D. 10

B. 5   E. $10\sqrt{2}$

C. $\dfrac{10\sqrt{2}}{2}$

138

Practice Test

1. In the figure below, △ ORS has one vertex at the center of a circle and two vertices on the circle. If ∠OSR measures 35°, what is the measure of ∠ROS?

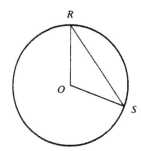

   A.   55°   D.   110°
   B.   90°   E.   145°
   C.   103°

2. In the figure below $\overline{UV}$ is parallel to $\overline{XY}$ and $\overline{UY}$ intersects $\overline{VX}$ at W. If the measure of ∠UVW is 30° and the measure of ∠WYX is 70°, what is the measure of ∠VWY?

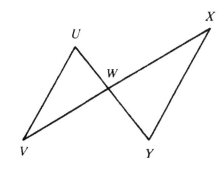

   A.   30°   D.   100°
   B.   70°   E.   110°
   C.   80°

3. Which polygon is not a parallelogram?

   A.   Square
   B.   Rhombus
   C.   Rectangle
   D.   Trapezoid
   E.   The polygon formed by joining the midpoints of any quadrilateral

4. What is the name of the polygon if the sum of the measures of its interior angles is 1080°?

   A.   Pentagon   D.   Decagon
   B.   Hexagon   E.   Dodecagon
   C.   Octagon

5. Which of the three triangles shown are congruent?

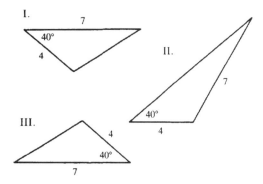

   A.   I and II only
   B.   I and III only
   C.   II and III only
   D.   I, II, III
   E.   No triangle is congruent to any other triangle.

6. A yardstick casts a 5-foot shadow at the same time that a tree casts a 75-foot shadow. How tall is the tree?

   A.   125 feet   D.   5 feet
   B.   75 feet   E.   None of the above
   C.   45 feet

7. In the figure, what is the length, in inches, of a side of square *ABCD*?

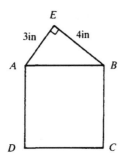

A.   5   D.   13
B.   6   E.   25
C.   12

8. If two sides of a right triangle have lengths of 1 and $\sqrt{2}$, which of the following could be the length of the third side?

    I.   1 inch
    II. 2 inches
    III. 3 inches

A.   I only   D.   I and II only
B.   II only   E.   I and III only
C.   III only

9. If each side of an equilateral triangle has a length of 12 units, what is the length of an altitude of the triangle?

A. $4\sqrt{3}$ D. $6\sqrt{3}$
B.   6   E.   None of the above
C. $6\sqrt{2}$

10. Find the perimeter of a square, in meters, that has a diagonal of length 20 meters.

A.   40   D. $80\sqrt{2}$
B. $40\sqrt{2}$ E.   100
C.   80

Basic Properties of a Circle: Radius, Diameter, and Circumference

A radius is a line segment joining the center of a circle and a point on the circle.

RADIUS

A diameter is a straight line passing through the center of the circle and terminating at two points on the circumference. It measures the distance across a circle, and its measure is equal to twice the measure of the radius.

DIAMETER

Circumference is the distance around a circle. It replaces the word perimeter in circles.

CIRCUMFERENCE

NOTE: No matter how large or small a circle is, the length of the diameter will always divide into the circumference the same number of times. This ratio is represented by the Greek letter π.

Approximate values for π are 3.14 and $\frac{22}{7}$.

The formula for finding the circumference is $C = \pi d$, where d is the diameter.

Concentric circles are circles that lie in the same plane and have the same center and radii of different length.

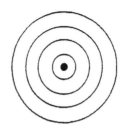

Example
Approximate the circumference of a circle with a diameter of 14 inches. Use $\frac{22}{7}$ as an approximation for π.

Solution
$C = \pi d$

$C = \frac{22}{7} \cdot \overset{2}{\cancel{14}}_{1}$

$C = 44$ inches

Example
Approximate the circumference of a circle with a radius of 21 inches. Use $\frac{22}{7}$ as an approximation for π.

Solution
$C = \pi d$

$C = \frac{22}{7} \cdot \overset{6}{\cancel{42}}_{1}$

$C = 132$ inches

Example
The circumference of a circle measures 66 feet. Approximate the radius of the circle. Use $\frac{22}{7}$ as an approximation for π.

Solution

$$C = \pi d$$

$$66 = \frac{22}{7} \cdot d$$

$$\left(\frac{7}{\cancel{22}_{1}}\right)\overset{3}{\cancel{66}} = \frac{\overset{1}{\cancel{22}}}{\cancel{7}}\left(\frac{\overset{1}{\cancel{7}}}{\cancel{22}_{1}}\right) \cdot d \qquad \text{(Multiplying both}$$

$$21 = d \qquad\qquad\qquad\qquad\quad \text{sides by } \frac{22}{7}\text{)}$$

The radius approximately equals $\frac{21}{2}$ or $10\frac{1}{2}$ feet.

<u>Other important definitions in relation to a circle</u>

Secant—A line drawn from a point outside a circle that intersects a circle in two points. See $\overline{AD}$ below.

Chord—A line segment joining any two points on the circle. (A diameter is a chord that passes through the center of the circle.) See $\overline{BA}$ below.

Tangent—a line that intersects a circle at one and *only* one point on the circumference. See $\overline{CD}$ below.

(If a line is tangent to a circle, it is perpendicular to the radius drawn to the point of tangency.)
$\overline{OC}$ is a radius.
Line CD is perpendicular to $\overline{OC}$ at point C.

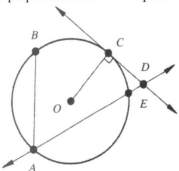

Circumference and Arc Length

Circumference of a Circle

The circumference of a circle is the entire length of the arc of a circle or the distance around the circle. In all circles, regardless of the size, the ratio $\dfrac{\text{circumference}}{\text{diameter}}$ is constant. This constant value is π.

Example
Find the circumference of a circle if the length of its radius is 5". (Use $\pi = 3.14$).

Solution
Since radius = 5, diameter = 10
$C = \pi d$
$C = (3.14)(10)$
$C = 31.4$"

Example
Sometimes it is necessary to find the length of an arc, which is equivalent to finding a fractional part of the circumference. In the figure, how can the length of $\overset{\frown}{AB}$ and the length of $\overset{\frown}{BC}$ be found?

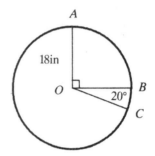

Solution
The first step is to find the circumference. If $r = 18$, then $d = 36$.
$C = \pi d$
$C = \pi \cdot 36$
$C = 36\pi$
The second step is to find the fractional part of the circumference contained in the length of the arc. Since $m\,\overset{\frown}{AB} = 90°$, it is $\dfrac{90}{360}$ or $\dfrac{1}{4}$ of the entire circle.

Therefore, $\overset{\frown}{AB} = \dfrac{1}{4} \cdot 36\pi = 9\pi$ inches.

Since $m\,\overset{\frown}{BC} = 20°$, it is $\dfrac{20}{360}$ or $\dfrac{1}{18}$ of the entire circle. $\overset{\frown}{BC} = \dfrac{1}{18} \cdot 36\pi = 2\pi$ inches.

The length of an arc can be found using the above procedure, which results in the formula

$$\text{Length of arc} = \frac{n}{360} \cdot \pi d$$

where n = number of degrees in the arc.

Example

O is the center of the circle with a radius of 4".
Find the length of $\overset{\frown}{AB}$ intercepted by a central angle of 40°.

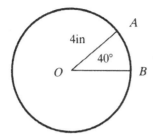

Solution

$\overset{\frown}{AB}$ contains 40° since it is intercepted by central $\angle AOB$, which measures 40°.

Using the formula

$$\text{length } \overset{\frown}{AB} = \frac{n}{360} \bullet \pi d$$

$$= \frac{40}{360} \bullet \pi \bullet 8$$

$$= \frac{8\pi}{9} \text{ inches}$$

Example

A wheel is rolled and makes five revolutions. If the diameter of the wheel is 3 feet, how far does the wheel travel?

Solution

As the wheel makes one revolution, every point on the wheel touches the ground. The distance the wheel travels during one revolution is the distance around the wheel (the circumference). In this exercise,

$$C = \pi d$$
$$C = \pi(3)$$
$$C = 3\pi \text{ feet}$$

Since there are five revolutions, multiply 3π by 5. The answer is 15π feet.

Measurement of Arcs

Central angle is an angle whose vertex is at the center of the circle.

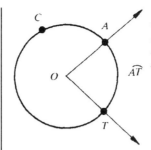

O is the center of the circle
$\angle AOT$ is a central angle
$\overset{\frown}{AT}$ is a minor arc
$\overset{\frown}{ACT}$ is a major arc

IMPORTANT:
The measure of a minor arc equals the measure of its central angle.
The measure of a semicircle is 180°.
The measure of a major arc is 360° minus the measure of the central angle's intercepted arc.

Example

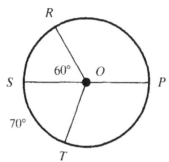

If $m \angle ROS = 60°$
$\quad m \overset{\frown}{ST} = 70°$
SP is a diameter
Then $\quad m \overset{\frown}{RS} = 60°$
$\quad m \overset{\frown}{RP} = 180° - 60° = 120°$
$\quad m \overset{\frown}{RT} = 60° + 70° = 130°$
$\quad m \overset{\frown}{STP} = 180°$
$\quad m \overset{\frown}{RPT} = 360° - 130° = 230°$

Example

O is the center; a central angle intercepts a minor arc of $x°$ and a major arc of $3x + 20°$. Find y.

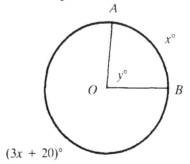

143

Solution

The sum of the measures of the minor and major arcs is 360°.

$x + (3x + 20) = 360$
$x + 3x + 20 = 360$ (simplifying terms)
$4x + 20 = 360$ (combining similar terms)
$-20 \quad -20$ (using the additive inverse)
$4x = 340$
$\frac{1}{4}(4x) = (340)\frac{1}{4}$ (using the multiplicative inverse)
$x = 85$

Since $\angle AOB$ is a central angle, $y = x = 85$.

Example

Given the three central angles, find the measure of minor arc y.

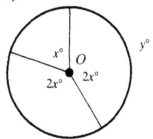

Solution

The three central angles intercept three arcs which form the entire circle = (360°). The equation would be:

$x + 2x + 2x = 360$
$5x = 360$ (combining similar terms)
$\frac{1}{5}(5x) = (360)\frac{1}{5}$ (using the multiplicative inverse)
$x = 72$

Since $y = 2x$, $y = 144°$.

Example

What is the measure of the obtuse angle formed by the two hands of a clock at 5 P.M.?

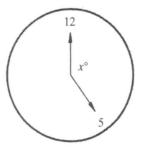

Solution

x is $\frac{5}{12}$ of 360.

$x = \frac{5}{\cancel{12}_{1}} \times \frac{\cancel{360}^{30}}{1}$

$x = 150°$

Example

O is the center. The measure of $\angle A$ is 62°. Find x.

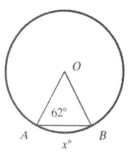

Solution

To find x, find the number of degrees in the central $\angle AOB$. OA and OB are radii in the same circle and are, therefore, equal. The angles opposite these equal sides are equal, so $m \angle B = 62°$.

$m \angle AOB + 62° + 62° = 180°$ (combining similar
$m \angle AOB + 124° = 180°$ terms)
$-124° - 124°$ (using the additive inverse)
$m \angle AOB = 56°$

Since central $\angle AOB$ measures 56°, its intercepted arc measures 56°.

Example (special case)

O is the center; $ABCDEF$ is a regular hexagon inscribed in the circle whose sides are eight units long. Find x.

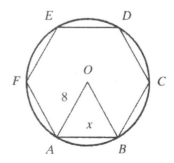

144

Solution

A regular hexagon is a polygon whose six sides and six angles are congruent. Its central angle measures 60° (360 ÷ 6 = 60°). Triangle *AOB* is isosceles and ∠*OAB* = ∠*OBA*. A regular hexagon contains 6 equilateral triangles.
Thus *x* = 8.

An **inscribed angle** is an angle whose vertex is on the circle and whose sides are chords of the circle. A chord is a line drawn within a circle touching two points on the circumference of the circle.

Example

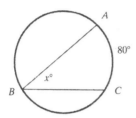

Angle *ABC* is an inscribed angle. The measure of an inscribed angle is equal to one-half the measure of its intercepted arc. If $m \widehat{AC} = 80$:

∠*x* measures $\frac{1}{2}(80)$; ∠*x* measures 40°.

Example
If the three arcs of the circle measure *x*°, *x*°, and (3*x* + 10)°, find inscribed ∠*y*.

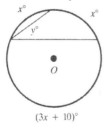

Solution
Find *x* by using the equation:

$x + x + (3x + 10) = 360$
$x + x + 3x + 10 = 360$ (simplifying terms)
$5x + 10 = 360$ (combining similar terms)
$\underline{\quad\quad -10 \quad -10}$ (using the additive inverse)
$5x = 350$

$\frac{1}{5}(5x) = (350)\frac{1}{5}$ (using the multiplicative inverse)

$x = 70°$

Since *y* is the measure of an inscribed angle, it measures $\frac{1}{2}(x) = 35°$

Example
O is the center. Find *x*.

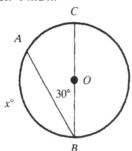

Solution
$\overline{BC}$ is a diameter (a chord that passes through the center of the circle forming 2 equal arcs of 180° each). Angle *B* is an inscribed angle. The measure of $\widehat{AC}$ is 60° and the measure of $\widehat{BAC}$ is 180°. Therefore:
$x + 60 = 180$
$\underline{\;-60 \quad -60}$ (using the additive inverse)
$x = 120$

Example
O is the center. Find *x*.

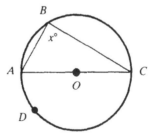

Solution
$\overline{AC}$ is a diameter and $\widehat{ADC}$ is a semi-circle whose measure is 180°.

$$x = \frac{1}{2} \; m \; \widehat{ADC}$$

$$x = \frac{1}{2}(180)$$

$$x = 90°$$

Note: Any angle inscribed in a semi-circle is a right angle.

145

Example

O is the center. Chords $\overline{BC}$ and $\overline{AC}$ form an inscribed angle of 30°. Find the central angle whose measure is x.

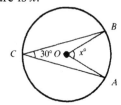

Solution

$$\angle C = \frac{1}{2} \ m \ \overset{\frown}{AB}$$

$$30° = \frac{1}{2} \ m \ \overset{\frown}{AB}$$

$2(30°) = (\frac{1}{2} \ m \ \overset{\frown}{AB})2$ (using the multiplicative inverse)

$$60° = m \ \overset{\frown}{AB}$$

$$x = m \ \overset{\frown}{AB}$$

$$x = 60°$$

Example

Inscribed $\angle CAD$ measures 50°. Find the inscribed angle whose measure is x.

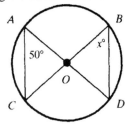

Solution

$$m \ \angle A = \frac{1}{2} \ m \ \overset{\frown}{CD}$$

$$50° = \frac{1}{2} \ m \ \overset{\frown}{CD}$$

$2(50°) = (\frac{1}{2} \ m \ \overset{\frown}{CD})2$ (using the multiplicative inverse)

$$100° = m \ \overset{\frown}{CD}$$

$$m \ \angle B = \frac{1}{2} \ m \ \overset{\frown}{CD}$$

$$m \ \angle B = \frac{1}{2}(100°)$$

$$m \ \angle B = 50°$$

Therefore, $x = 50°$

The measures of two inscribed angles are equal if they intercept the same arc.

Areas of Circles, Triangles, Rectangles, Parallelograms, Trapezoids, and Other Figures with Formulas

Besides the circle, the most important polygons are the triangles and the quadrilaterals.

Following is a list of area formulas you should memorize with accompanying examples.

Circle

Area $= \pi r^2$

$\quad\quad = \pi \bullet 5^2$

$\quad\quad = 25\pi$

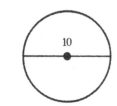

Rectangle

Area $= bh$

$\quad\quad = 8 \bullet 3$

$\quad\quad = 24$

Parallelogram

Area $= bh$

$\quad\quad = 9 \bullet 4$

$\quad\quad = 36$

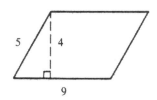

Rhombus

Area $= \frac{1}{2}$ product of diagonals

$\quad\quad = \frac{1}{2} d_1 d_2$, which is a special case of a parallelogram

If $RT = 10$, $US = 24$

Area $= \frac{1}{2} \bullet 10 \bullet 24$

$\quad\quad = 120$

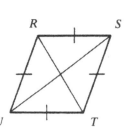

Square

Area $= s^2$

$\quad\quad = 7^2$

$\quad\quad = 49$

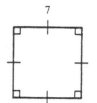

146

Trapezoid

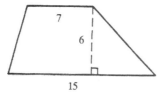

Area $= \dfrac{1}{2} h(b_1 + b_2)$ where h = altitude and b_1

                         and b_2 are the lengths of
                         the parallel bases

$= \dfrac{1}{2} \bullet 6(15 + 7)$

$= \dfrac{1}{2} \bullet 6 \bullet 22$

$= 66$

Triangle

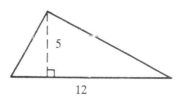

Area $= \dfrac{1}{2} bh$

$= \dfrac{1}{2} \bullet 12 \bullet 5$

$= 30$

Right Triangle

Area $= \dfrac{1}{2}$ product of legs

$= \dfrac{1}{2} \bullet 6 \bullet 8$

$= 24$

Equilateral Triangle

Area $= \dfrac{s^2\sqrt{3}}{4}$ where s = length of a side

$= \dfrac{2^2\sqrt{3}}{4}$

$= \dfrac{4\sqrt{3}}{4}$

$= \sqrt{3}$

A sector of a circle is the region bounded by an arc of the circle and two radii drawn to the endpoints of the arc.

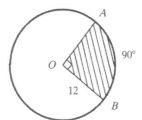

Area of sector $= \dfrac{n}{360} \bullet \pi r^2$ where n equals

degree measure of the arc of the sector.

$$\begin{aligned} \text{Area of sector } OAB &= \dfrac{n}{360} \bullet \pi r^2 \\ &= \dfrac{90}{360} \bullet \pi \bullet 12^2 \\ &= \dfrac{90}{360} \bullet \pi \bullet 12 \bullet 12 \\ &= 36\pi \text{ square units} \end{aligned}$$

Computing the area of a specified region

Example
What is the area of the shaded portion?

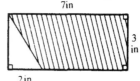

Solution
The area of the shaded portion equals the area of the rectangle minus the area of the triangle. Area of rectangle = length × width = 7" × 3" = 21 square inches. Area of triangle $= \dfrac{1}{2}$ × base × height $= \dfrac{1}{2}$ × 2" × 3" = 3 square inches. Area of shaded region = 21 square inches – 3 square inches = 18 square inches. To solve this problem: (1) Find the area of the outside, larger figure; (2) Find the area of the smaller, undefined figure; (3) Subtract the area of the unshaded figure from the area of the outside larger figure.

Orientation Exercises

1. Following are the distances, in feet, of five points from the center of a circle.

   Point R—2.75   Point U—3.00
   Point S—3.01   Point V—2.50
   Point T—2.01

   If the diameter of the circle is 6 feet, which point lies outside the circle?

   A.   Point R   D.   Point U
   B.   Point S   E.   Point V
   C.   Point T

2. When the circumference of a circle is increased from 10π inches to 15π inches, by how many inches is the radius increased?

   A.   20   D.   5
   B.   10   E. $2\frac{1}{2}$
   C. $7\frac{1}{2}$

3. In the figure, $m \angle AOC = 48°$ in the circle centered at O. Find $m \angle ABC$.

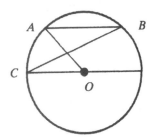

   A.   96   D.   24
   B.   72   E.   None of the above
   C.   48

4. In the figure, O is the center of the circle. If $m \angle RST = 30°$ and $\overline{TW}$ is tangent to the circle at point T, what is the measure of $\angle TWO$?

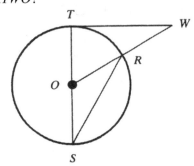

   A.   15°   D.   60°
   B.   30°   E.   75°
   C.   45°

5. In the figure, find the area, in square meters, of the entire region formed by $\triangle ABC$ and the semicircle having AB as its diameter.

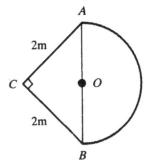

   A. $2 + \pi$ D. $4 + 4\pi$
   B. $2 + 2\pi$ E. $2 + 4\pi$
   C. $1 + \pi$

6. Find the area of a sector of a circle if the sector has a central angle of 90° and a radius of 2 units.

   A.   1   D. 4π
   B. π E.   8
   C. 2π

148

Practice Exercises

1. In the diagram, which line segment is a diameter?

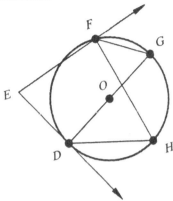

   A. $\overline{DH}$ D. $\overline{DE}$
   B. $\overline{DO}$ E. $\overline{FH}$
   C. $\overline{DG}$

2. If a radius of a circle is doubled, what happens to the circumference of the new circle?
   A. It remains the same.
   B. It is halved.
   C. It is doubled.
   D. It equals π.
   E. It equals 2π.

3. In the figure below, $\angle XYZ$ is inscribed in circle O and $m \ \overset{\frown}{XZ} = 60°$. What is the measure of $\angle XYZ$?

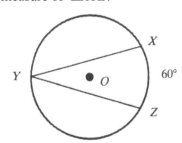

   A. 20° D. 120°
   B. 30° E. None of the above
   C. 60°

4. O is the center. $\overline{AB} \parallel \overline{CD}$. Find y.

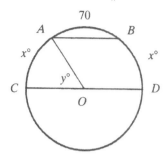

   A. $24\frac{1}{2}°$ D. 110°
   B. 55° E. None of the above
   C. 60°

5. In the figure, points R, S, and T are on the same line, and $\overline{RS}$ and $\overline{ST}$ are each 12 units long. If the area of $\triangle RWT$ is 48 square units, how long is altitude $\overline{SW}$?

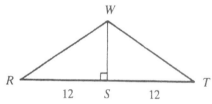

   A. 2 D. 12
   B. 4 E. 24
   C. 8

6. In the trapezoid shown, the perimeter equals 45, $BC = 9$, and $AD = 6$. Find the area.

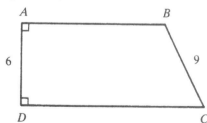

   A. $7\frac{1}{2}$ D. 180
   B. 18 E. $607\frac{1}{2}$
   C. 90

Practice Test

1. In the figure, ΔRST is inscribed in circle O. If RS = 6 units and ST = 8 units, then the length of the radius of the circle is:

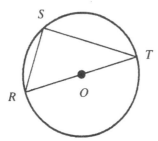

A. 5
B. 7
above
C. 10

D. 14
E. None of the

2. In the figure, $\overline{AB}$ is tangent to the circle centered at O at A. If AO = 2 units and m∠AOB = 60°, what is the length of $\overline{DB}$?

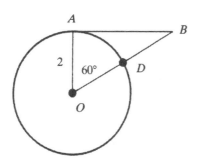

A. 2
B. $2\sqrt{3}$
C. 4

D. $4\sqrt{3}$
E. $4 - \sqrt{3}$

3. A wheel is rolled and makes 12 revolutions. If the radius of the wheel is 1.5 feet, how far does the wheel travel?

A. 8π feet
B. 18 feet
C. 18π feet

D. 36 feet
E. 36π feet

4. Circle O has a radius of r. An 8" chord intercepts 60° arc $\overset{\frown}{AB}$. Find the length, in inches, of $\overset{\frown}{AB}$.

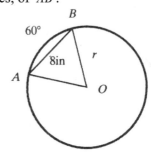

A. 8 inches
B. 16 inches
C. 8π inches

D. $\dfrac{8\pi}{3}$ inches
E. $\dfrac{16\pi}{3}$ inches

5. Justin has a rectangular piece of wood as shown in the diagram. If he cuts off the triangular shaped section in the corner, what is the ratio of the area removed to the area of the remaining piece?

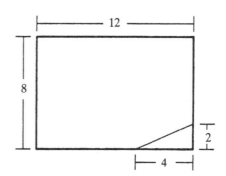

A. $\dfrac{1}{23}$
B. $\dfrac{1}{24}$
C. $\dfrac{1}{11}$

D. $\dfrac{1}{12}$
E. $\dfrac{1}{6}$

TRIGONOMETRY
SKILL BUILDER FOURTEEN

Right Triangle Trigonometry

The following six ratios are called the trigonometric functions of the acute angle.

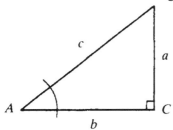

Use the following abbreviations
opp – length of opposite side
adj = length of adjacent side
hyp = length of hypotenuse

Reciprocal Relationships

$$\begin{array}{ll} \sin \angle A = \dfrac{\text{opp}}{\text{hyp}} = \dfrac{a}{c} & \sin \angle A = \dfrac{1}{\csc A} \\[2mm] \cos \angle A = \dfrac{\text{adj}}{\text{hyp}} = \dfrac{b}{c} & \cos \angle A = \dfrac{1}{\sec A} \\[2mm] \tan \angle A = \dfrac{\text{opp}}{\text{adj}} = \dfrac{a}{b} & \tan \angle A = \dfrac{1}{\cot A} \\[2mm] \cot \angle A = \dfrac{\text{adj}}{\text{opp}} = \dfrac{b}{a} & \cot \angle A = \dfrac{1}{\tan A} \\[2mm] \sec \angle A = \dfrac{\text{hyp}}{\text{adj}} = \dfrac{c}{b} & \sec \angle A = \dfrac{1}{\cos A} \\[2mm] \csc \angle A = \dfrac{\text{hyp}}{\text{opp}} = \dfrac{c}{a} & \csc \angle A = \dfrac{1}{\sin A} \end{array}$$

R E C I P R O C A L S

Trigonometric Functions of Angles of 30°, 45°, and 60°

NOTE: These values are used repeatedly in problems, and you can save a great deal of time if you memorize these values. It is not necessary to memorize the decimal values of these functions, but it might help.

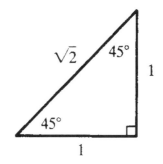

$$\sin 45° = \frac{1}{\sqrt{2}} = \frac{2\sqrt{2}}{2} \approx 0.707$$

$$\cos 45° = \frac{1}{\sqrt{2}} = \frac{2\sqrt{2}}{2} \approx 0.707$$

$$\tan 45° = \frac{1}{1} = 1$$

$$\cot 45° = \frac{1}{1} = 1$$

$$\sec 45° = \frac{\sqrt{2}}{1} = \sqrt{2} \approx 1.414$$

$$\csc 45° = \frac{\sqrt{2}}{1} = \sqrt{2} \approx 1.414$$

Some Commonly Used Square Roots

$\sqrt{2} \approx 1.414$	$\sqrt{64} = 8$
$\sqrt{3} \approx 1.732$	$\sqrt{81} = 9$
$\sqrt{4} = 2$	$\sqrt{100} = 10$
$\sqrt{9} = 3$	$\sqrt{121} = 11$
$\sqrt{16} = 4$	$\sqrt{144} = 12$
$\sqrt{25} = 5$	$\sqrt{225} = 15$
$\sqrt{36} = 6$	$\sqrt{400} = 20$
$\sqrt{49} = 7$	$\sqrt{625} = 25$

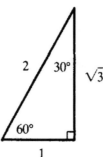

$$\sin 60° = \frac{\sqrt{3}}{2} \approx 0.866$$

$$\cos 60° = \frac{1}{2} = 0.500$$

$$\tan 60° = \frac{\sqrt{3}}{1} \approx 1.732$$

$$\cot 60° = \frac{1}{\sqrt{3}} = \frac{\sqrt{3}}{3} \approx 0.5774$$

$$\sec 60° = \frac{2}{1} = 2$$

$$\csc 60° = \frac{2}{\sqrt{3}} = \frac{2\sqrt{3}}{3} \approx 1.155$$

$$\sin 30° = \frac{1}{2} = 0.500$$

$$\cos 30° = \frac{\sqrt{3}}{2} \approx 0.866$$

$$\tan 30° = \frac{1}{\sqrt{3}} = \frac{\sqrt{3}}{3} \approx 0.577$$

$$\cot 30° = \frac{\sqrt{3}}{1} = \sqrt{3} \approx 1.732$$

$$\sec 30° = \frac{2}{\sqrt{3}} = \frac{2\sqrt{3}}{3} \approx 1.155$$

$$\csc 30° = \frac{2}{1} = 2$$

If you know the value of one trigonometric function, you can easily construct the angle and write the value of its five other trigonometric functions.

Example

If $\angle A$ is an acute angle and $\sin A = \frac{3}{5}$, find $\tan A$.

Solution

1. Construct the angle $\sin A = \frac{3}{5} = \frac{\text{opp}}{\text{hyp}}$

2. Find the third side

3. Tan equals $\frac{\text{opp}}{\text{adj}}$

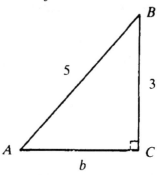

$$5^2 = 3^2 + b^2$$
$$25 = 9 + b^2$$
$$16 = b^2$$
$$4 = b$$

Thus, $\tan A = \frac{\text{opp}}{\text{adj}} = \frac{3}{4}$

Example
Evaluate $\sin 45° \cdot \cos 60°$.

Solution
Substitute the trigonometric function values:
$$\sin 45° \cdot \cos 60°$$
$$\frac{\sqrt{2}}{2} \cdot \frac{1}{2} = \frac{\sqrt{2}}{4}$$

Example
A kite has 80 meters of string out. The string makes an angle of 30° with the ground. How far above the ground is the kite?

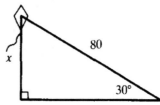

Solution

$\sin 30° = \dfrac{x}{80}$ $80 \cdot \dfrac{1}{2} = x$

$80 \cdot \sin 30° = x$ $40 \text{ meters} = x$

Trigonometric Identities

There are eight fundamental relationships. These relationships among the trigonometric functions are extremely important in more advanced courses in mathematics.

The first group is called the **reciprocal** relationships.

θ = Greek letter "theta"

$$\sin \theta = \frac{1}{\csc \theta}$$

$$\cos \theta = \frac{1}{\sec \theta}$$

$$\tan \theta = \frac{1}{\cot \theta}$$

The second group is called the **ratio** relationships.

$$\tan \theta = \frac{\sin \theta}{\cos \theta}$$

$$\cot \theta = \frac{\cos \theta}{\sin \theta}$$

The third group is called the **Pythagorean** relationships.

$$\sin^2 \theta = \cos^2 \theta = 1$$
$$\tan^2 \theta + 1 = \sec^2 \theta$$
$$1 + \cot^2 \theta = \csc^2 \theta$$

Example
Simplify $\cos A \tan A$, when $\cos A \neq 0$.

Solution
Substitute $\frac{\sin A}{\cos A}$ for $\tan A$

$$\cos A \tan A$$

$$\overset{1}{\cancel{\cos A}} \cdot \frac{\sin A}{\underset{1}{\cancel{\cos A}}}$$

$$\sin A$$

Example
Simplify $\tan^2 \theta \cos^2 \theta \csc \theta$.

Solution

$$\frac{\sin^2 \theta}{\cos^2 \theta} \cdot \cos^2 \theta \cdot \frac{1}{\sin \theta}$$

$$\frac{\overset{\sin \theta}{\cancel{\sin^2 \theta}}}{\underset{1}{\cancel{\cos^2 \theta}}} \cdot \overset{1}{\cancel{\cos^2 \theta}} \cdot \frac{1}{\underset{1}{\cancel{\sin \theta}}}$$

$$\sin \theta$$

Addition Formulas for Sine and Cosine

The following formulas will involve the sum of two angles and are referred to as the multiple-angle formulas.

α = Greek letter "alpha"
β = Greek letter "beta"

Expressed in words: The sine of the sum of two angles equals the sine of the first angle times the cosine of the second angle plus the cosine of the first angle times the sine of the second angle.

Memorize: $\sin(\alpha + \beta) = \sin \alpha \cos \beta + \cos \alpha \sin \beta$

Example
Find the value of $\sin(30° + 45°)$.

Solution
Expand the formula:
$\sin(30° + 45°) = \sin 30° \cos 45° + \cos 30° \sin 45°$
Substitute values:

$$= \frac{1}{2} \cdot \frac{\sqrt{2}}{2} + \frac{\sqrt{3}}{2} \cdot \frac{\sqrt{2}}{2}$$

$$= \frac{\sqrt{2}}{4} + \frac{\sqrt{6}}{4}$$

$$= \frac{\sqrt{2} + \sqrt{6}}{4}$$

Expressed in words: The cosine of the sum of two angles equals the product of their cosines minus the product of their sines.

Memorize: $\cos(\alpha + \beta) = \cos \alpha \cos \beta - \sin \alpha \sin \beta$

Example
Find the value of $\cos(30 + 45°)$.

Solution

Expand the formula:

cos(30° + 45°) = cos 30° cos 45° – sin 30° sin 45°

Substitute values:

$$= \frac{\sqrt{3}}{2} \cdot \frac{\sqrt{2}}{2} - \frac{1}{2} \cdot \frac{\sqrt{2}}{2}$$

$$= \frac{\sqrt{6}}{4} + \frac{\sqrt{2}}{4}$$

$$= \frac{\sqrt{6} + \sqrt{2}}{4}$$

Graphs of Trigonometric Functions, Including Amplitude, Period, and Phase Shift

Table method graphing or using unit circle and projecting points will produce the following graphs of the six trigonometric ratios.

All the trigonometric functions have the property of repeating their values in an interval of length 2π. Functions having this property are called **periodic functions**.

The length of the maximum ordinate of the trigonometric function is called the **amplitude** of the function. It is the coefficient of the trigonometric function.

The **period** of the function is the length of the interval in which the trigonometric function repeats itself.

In general, given an equation $y = a \sin bx$, the amplitude equals a and the period is $\frac{2\pi}{b}$.

$y = \sin \theta$
amplitude = 1
period = 360°

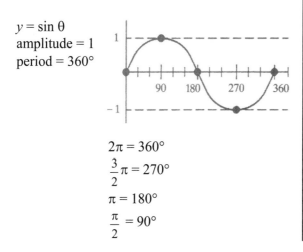

$$2\pi = 360°$$
$$\frac{3}{2}\pi = 270°$$
$$\pi = 180°$$
$$\frac{\pi}{2} = 90°$$

$y = \cos \theta$
amplitude = 1
period = 2π

$y = \tan \theta$
amplitude = none
period = π

$y = \cot \theta$
amplitude = none
period = π

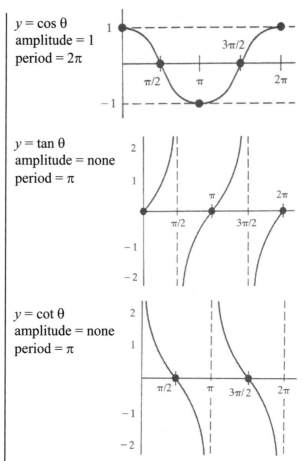

The dashed lines are asymptotes. The graph of the function approaches these dashed vertical lines but never reaches them.

$y = \sec \theta$
amplitude = none
period = 2π

$y = \csc \theta$
amplitude = none
period = 2π

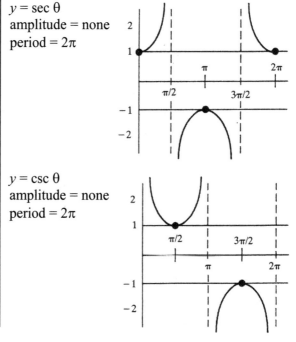

154

Example

Draw the graph of $y = 2 \sin \dfrac{1}{2} x.$

Solution

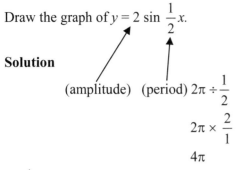

(amplitude)   (period) $2\pi \div \dfrac{1}{2}$

$2\pi \times \dfrac{2}{1}$

4π

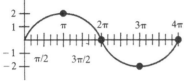

Example

Draw the graph of $y = \dfrac{3}{2} \cos 2\theta,$

Solution

amplitude $= \dfrac{3}{2}$

period $= 2\pi \div 2$

$2\pi \bullet \dfrac{1}{2} = \dfrac{2\pi}{2} = \pi$

Phase Shift

We say that $\sin x$ and $\cos x$ are periodic functions with period 360°, and they repeat themselves every 360°. The same graphs for $\sin x$ and $\cos x$ are obtained when x is measured in the angular unit radian.

NOTE: When sketching graphs of the trigonometric functions, let one unit on the horizontal scale equal 30° and two units on the vertical scale equal 1 because 1 radian $\approx 57.3°$.

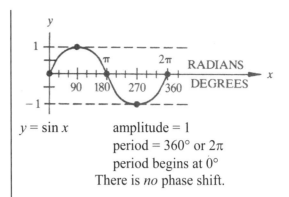

$y = \sin x$ amplitude $= 1$
period $= 360°$ or 2π
period begins at 0°
There is *no* phase shift.

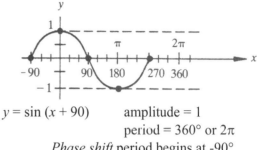

$y = \sin (x + 90)$ amplitude $= 1$
period $= 360°$ or 2π
Phase shift period begins at -90°
and completes one cycle at 270°

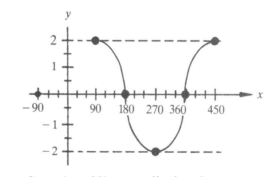

$y = 2 \cos (x - 90)$ amplitude $= 2$
period $= 360°$ or 2π
Phase shift period begins at 90°
and completes one cycle at 450°

The graph of any equation of the form
$y = a \sin(x + b)$ or $y = a \cos(x + b)$ for a given real number b may be obtained by setting $x + b = 0$ to find the starting point of the curve.

Orientation Exercises

1. The lengths of the sides of the triangle shown are 5, 12, and 13 units and A is the measure of one of the angles, as indicated in the figure. What is the $\cos A$?

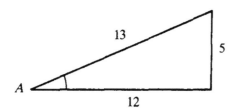

   A. $\dfrac{5}{13}$ D. $\dfrac{12}{5}$

   B. $\dfrac{5}{12}$ E. $\dfrac{13}{5}$

   C. $\dfrac{12}{13}$

2. In $\triangle RST$, the measures of $\angle R$, $\angle S$, and $\angle T$ are 90°, 55°, and 35°, respectively. If $\overline{TR}$ is 6 units long, how many units long is $\overline{SR}$?

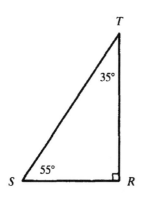

   A. 8   D. 6 tan 35°

   B. 10   E. 6 tan 55°

   C. tan 20°

3. Simplify $\sec^2 \theta - \tan^2 \theta$

   A. $2\cos^2 \theta$ D. $1 - \cos^2 \theta$

   B. $1 - \sin^2 \theta$ E. $2 \sin \theta$

   C. 1

4. Simplify $\dfrac{\sin^2 x}{1 - \sin^2 x}$

   A. -1 D. $\tan^2 x$

   B. 0   E. $\cot^2 x$

   C. 1

5. Find the value of $\sin(60° + 45°)$.

   A. $\dfrac{\sqrt{6} + \sqrt{2}}{4}$

   B. $\dfrac{\sqrt{6} - \sqrt{2}}{4}$

   C. $\dfrac{\sqrt{2} - \sqrt{6}}{4}$

   D. 1

   E. None of the above

6. $\cos 135° \cos 30° - \sin 135° \sin 30° = ?$

   A. $\cos 105°$ D. $\cos 165°$

   B. $\sin 105°$ E. $\cos 330°$

   C. $\sin 165°$

7. In the equation $y = a \cos b\theta$, where θ is in radians, $\dfrac{2\pi}{b}$ is the:

   A. amplitude
   B. pitch
   C. inclination of the curve
   D. period
   E. phase shift

8. The period of $y = \dfrac{3}{2} \cos 4\theta$, where θ is in radians, is:

   A. $\dfrac{3}{2}$ D. 4π

   B. $\dfrac{\pi}{2}$ E. 6π

   C. π

156

Practice Exercises

1. Evaluate $2 \sin 30° - \tan 45° + 60°$

   A. 1
   B. 2
   C. 3
   D. $\sqrt{2} + 1$
   E. $\sqrt{2} + 2$

2. If $\sin x = \dfrac{1}{2}$, what does $\tan x = ?$

   A. $\dfrac{\sqrt{2}}{3}$
   B. $\sqrt{3}$
   C. $\dfrac{\sqrt{3}}{3}$
   D. $\dfrac{\sqrt{2}}{2}$
   E. $\dfrac{1}{4}$

3. Simplify $\dfrac{\cos x}{\csc x} + \cos^2 x \tan x$.

   A. $2 \sin x \cos x$
   B. $(\sin x)(\cos x + 1)$
   C. 1
   D. $\tan x + \cos x \sin x$
   E. $\sin x + \cos x \sin x$

4. Simplify $\cot A \cos A \tan A$.

   A. $\dfrac{1}{\cos A}$
   B. $\cos A$
   C. $\dfrac{1}{\sin A}$
   D. $\sin A$
   E. $\sec A$

5. Find the value of $\cos(45° + 60°)$.

   A. $\dfrac{\sqrt{6} + \sqrt{2}}{4}$
   B. $\dfrac{\sqrt{6} - \sqrt{2}}{4}$
   C. $\dfrac{\sqrt{2} - \sqrt{6}}{4}$
   D. 1
   E. 0

6. If $\sin \alpha = \dfrac{3}{5}$ and $\cos \beta = \dfrac{12}{13}$ and α and β are in quadrant I, then what is the value of $\sin (\alpha + \beta)$?

   A. 0
   B. $\dfrac{20}{65}$
   C. $\dfrac{36}{65}$
   D. $\dfrac{56}{65}$
   E. 1

7. As θ increases from $0°$ to $90°$, which of the following is true?

   A. $\sin \theta$ decreases
   B. $\cos \theta$ increases
   C. $\tan \theta$ decreases
   D. $\csc \theta$ increases
   E. $\sec \theta$ increases

8. The amplitude of $y = \sin \dfrac{1}{2} \theta$ is:

   A. 4
   B. 2
   C. 1
   D. $\dfrac{1}{2}$
   E. It has no amplitude.

157

Practice Test

1. If the sine of an angle in quadrant I is $\frac{4}{5}$, what is the cosine of the angle?

   A. $\frac{3}{5}$ D. $\frac{\sqrt{3}}{2}$

   B. $\frac{1}{5}$ E. $\frac{\sqrt{2}}{2}$

   C. $\frac{5}{3}$

2. What is the length, in inches, of the hypotenuse of $\triangle ABC$?

   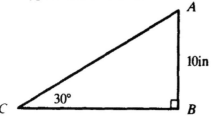

   A. 12   D. 5
   B. $10\sqrt{2}$ E. 50
   C. 20

   A. 12   D. 5
   B. $10\sqrt{2}$ E. 50
   C. 20

3. If $\sin A = \frac{1}{2}$ amd $\cos A = \frac{\sqrt{3}}{2}$, then $\tan A = ?$

   A. $\frac{\sqrt{3}}{4}$ D. $\frac{3}{\sqrt{3}}$

   B. $\sqrt{3}$ E. $\frac{\sqrt{3}}{3}$

   C. 3

4. For all θ, which of the following is NOT an identity?

   A. $\cos \theta = \frac{1}{\sec \theta}$

   B. $\cot \theta = \frac{\cos \theta}{\sin \theta}$

   C. $\sin \theta \bullet \csc \theta = 1$
   D. $1 + \cot^2 \theta = \csc^2 \theta$
   E. $\sin \theta + \cos \theta = 1$

5. $\cos 45° \cos 30° - \sin 45° \sin 30° = ?$

   A. $\cos 150°$ D. $\sin 75°$
   B. $\cos\ 75°$ E. $\sin 15°$
   C. $\cos\ 15°$

6. If $\sin \alpha = \frac{3}{5}$ and $\cos \beta = \frac{3}{5}$ and α and β are in quadrant I, then what is the value of $\sin (\alpha + \beta)$?

   A. $\frac{6}{5}$ D. $\frac{7}{25}$

   B. 1   E. $\frac{1}{5}$

   C. $\frac{14}{25}$

7. Comparing the graphs of $y = \cos \theta$ and $y = 4 \cos \theta$, you can conclude that for the second function, the:

   A. period is twice as great.
   B. amplitude is one-half as great.
   C. period is four times as great.
   D. amplitude is four times as great.
   E. period is one-half as great.

8. The trigonometric function of 275° that has the greatest positive value is:

   A. cosine   D. secant
   B. tangent   E. cosecant
   C. cotangent

1. In the graph below, what is the slope of line *k*?

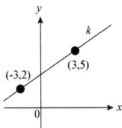

A. - 2

B. $-\frac{1}{2}$

C. $\frac{1}{8}$

D. $\frac{1}{2}$

E. 2

2. Given any positive fraction with the numerator less than the denominator, the decimal equivalent of that fraction:

F. is always less than 1.
G. may equal 1, but cannot be greater than 1.
H. is sometimes greater than 1.
J. is always either equal to 1 or is greater than 1.
K. is always greater than 1.

3. If $x + y = 14$ and $-x + 2y = 4$, then $x =$

A. -24   D. 8
B. -4   E. 16
C. 4

4. In a certain city, the assessed value of a house is 40% of the house's market value, and the property tax is 3.8% of the assessed value. What is the property tax on a home with a market value of $60,000?

F. $ 152.00   J. $2,280.00
G. $ 912.00   K. $9,120.00
H. $1,520.00

5. If (a, b) are the (x, y) coordinates of any point in the rectangular shaded region in the figure below, or on its boundary, what is the smallest possible value of $\frac{1}{a+b}$?

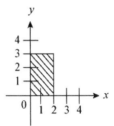

A. $\frac{1}{6}$ D. $\frac{1}{2}$

B. $\frac{1}{5}$ E. $\frac{5}{6}$

C. $\frac{1}{3}$

6. The (x, y) coordinates of points A, B, and C below are $(2, 3)$, $(3, 2)$, and $(1, 1)$, respectively. If $\triangle ABC$ is translated (slid) so that A's new coordinates are $(4, 3)$ and B's are $(5, 2)$, what are the new coordinates of C?

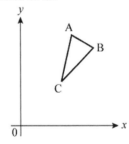

F. (1, 1)
G. (3, 1)
H. (1, 3)
J. (3, 3)
K. (3, 4)

7. In the figure below, △OBA has one vertex at the center of a circle and two vertices on the circle. If ∠OAB measures 24°, what is the measure of ∠BOA?

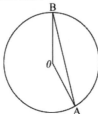

A. 66°
B. 90°
C. 114°
D. 132°
E. 156°

8. In the figure below, square *ABCD* with center at *E* is overlapped by square *EFGH*. If the area of *ABCD* is 144 square units, what is the area in square units of quadrilateral *EICJ*?

F. 12
G. 24
H. 36
J. 44
K. 72

9. The lengths of the sides of the triangle below are 3, 4, and 5 units, and *a* is the measure of one of the angles, as indicated in the figure. What is sin *a*?

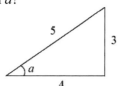

A. $\dfrac{3}{5}$
B. $\dfrac{3}{4}$
C. $\dfrac{4}{5}$
D. $\dfrac{4}{3}$
E. $\dfrac{5}{3}$

10. In △*ABC* below, the measures of ∠*ACB*, ∠*CBA*, and ∠*BAC* are 90°, 50°, and 40°, respectively. If $\overline{CB}$ is 4 units long, how many units long is $\overline{AC}$?

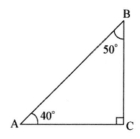

F. 3
G. 5
H. tan 10°
J. 4 tan 40°
K. 4 tan 50°

11. What is the equation of the ellipse graphed below?

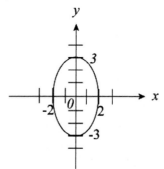

A. $\dfrac{y^2}{6} - \dfrac{x^2}{4} = 1$

B. $\dfrac{x^2}{4} - \dfrac{y^2}{6} = 1$

C. $\dfrac{x^2}{4} - \dfrac{y^2}{9} = 1$

D. $\dfrac{x^2}{4} + \dfrac{y^2}{9} = 1$

E. $\dfrac{x^2}{4} + \dfrac{y^2}{6} = 1$

12. $(3x^2 - 7x - 6) + (-3x + 2) = ?$

F. $3x^2 - 10x - 4$
G. $3x^2 - 4x - 4$
H. $3x^2 - 10x - 8$
J. $3x^2 - 4x - 8$
K. $3x^2 + 4x - 8$

160

13. $(2^4)^3 = ?$

A. $2\dfrac{4}{3}$
B. 2^7
C. 2^{12}
D. 2^{43}
E. 2^{64}

14. If the sum of four numbers is 0, and the three numbers are 23.86, -14.67, and 19.42, what is the fourth number?

F. -28.61
G. -27.61
H. 27.61
J. 28.61
K. 29.61

15. A six-sided die with the sides numbered 1 to 6 is tossed at the same time that a fair coin is flipped. A typical outcome is (5, H)—a 5 on the die and a head on the coin. How many different outcomes are possible?

A. 8
B. 12
C. 32
D. 36
E. 64

16. The cost, c, in dollars to order n picture frames is given by the formula $c = 4n + p$, where p is a constant equal to 5. How much does it cost to order three of these picture frames?

F. $12
G. $17
H. $19
J. $23
K. $60

17. The formula $I = prt$ can be used to calculate the simple interest earned on a principal p invested at the rate r per year for t years. Which of the following equations determines the number of years t that $100 must be invested for 8% per year until it has earned $80 in simple interest?

A. $20 = 80(0.08)t$
B. $20 = 100(0.08)t$
C. $80 = 100(0.08)t$
D. $100 = 80(0.08)t$
E. $180 = 100(0.08)t$

18. If the length and width of a rectangle are each doubled, then the perimeter of the new rectangle is how many times as large as the perimeter of the original rectangle?

F. 2
G. 3
H. 4
J. 6
K. 8

19. In the figure below, transversal line l_3 intersects parallel lines l_1 and l_2, and the measure of $\angle 1$ is twice the measure of $\angle 2$. What is the sum of the measures of $\angle 1$, $\angle 3$, $\angle 5$, and $\angle 7$?

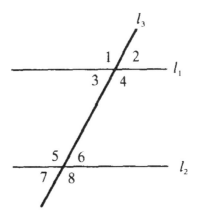

A. 180°
B. 240°
C. 360°
D. 480°
E. 720°

20. If a bowler has scores of 148 and 186 in the first two of three games, what must she score in the third game to have an average (arithmetic mean) score of exactly 172 for the three-game match?

F. 61
G. 112
H. 167
J. 172
K. 182

161

21. Eric gave half his money to Carly. Later, Eric gave half his remaining money to Helen. Eric's father then gave Eric an additional sum of money three times as large as the amount Eric had left. How does the total Eric now has compare with the amount he originally had?

A. It is $\dfrac{1}{12}$ as large as the original amount.

B. It is $\dfrac{3}{4}$ as large as the original amount.

C. It is the same as the original amount.

D. It is $\dfrac{3}{2}$ as large as the original amount.

E. It is 12 times as large as the original amount.

22. Which of the following is a prime number?

F. 21
G. 27
H. 31
J. 51
K. 91

23. In the figure below, A, D, and B are collinear and $\overline{AC}$ is perpendicular to $\overline{BC}$. If the measure of $\angle CAD$ is 30°, and the measure of $\angle DCB$ is 50°, what is the measure of $\angle ADC$?

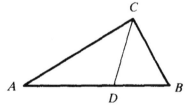

A. 110°
B. 120°
C. 130°
D. 140°
E. 150°

24. Which of the following equations has the solution set (5, -2)?

F. $x - 5 = 0$
G. $x + 2 = 0$
H. $x^2 = -10$
J. $x^2 - 3x - 10 = 0$
K. $x^2 + 3x - 10 = 0$

25. The sum of three numbers is 86. The second number is 5 more than the first number, and the third number is 5 times the second number. If the first number is represented by x, which of the following equations determines the correct value of x?

A. $x + (x + 5) + 5x = 86$
B. $x + (x + 5) + 5(x + 5) = 86$
C. $(x - 5) + x + 5x = 86$
D. $(x)(x + 5)(5x) = 86$
E. $(x)(x + 5)(x + 5) = 86$

26. After the price of a $12 shirt was reduced by 25%, it was then raised by 25% of the reduced price. What was the price of the shirt after these 2 price changes?

F. $12.00
G. $11.25
H. $9.00
J. $7.20
K. $6.75

27. The measures of four of the angles of pentagon $ABCDE$ are indicated on the figure below. What is the measure of the interior angle at E?

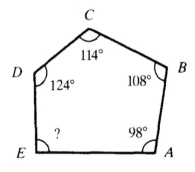

A. 69°
B. 96°
C. 98°
D. 108°
E. 111°

28. $\dfrac{(6!)}{(2!) \bullet (3!)} = ?$

F. 0
G. 1
H. 6
J. 60
K. 120

162

29. As shown in the chart below, the values of y are a linear function of the values of x. Which of the following computations determines the value of y when $x = 4$?

x	1	2	3	4	5
y	.81	1.41	2.01		3.21

A. $\dfrac{2.01-1.41}{2}$ D. $\dfrac{2.01+1.41}{2}$

B. $\dfrac{3.21-2.01}{2}$ E. $\dfrac{2.01+3.21}{2}$

C. $3.21 - 2.01$

30. The value of 2 is what percent of 2.5?

F. 20% J. 80%
G. 50% K. 125%
H. 75%

31. If $\dfrac{2}{y} + \dfrac{3}{2y} = 14$, then $y = ?$

A. 49   B. $\dfrac{5}{28}$ C. $\dfrac{1}{4}$

D. 4   E. $\dfrac{5}{42}$

32. $\overline{AB}$ is a diameter of the circle below; $\overline{BT}$ is tangent to the circle at B; and $\overline{AT}$ intersects the circle at C. If the measure of $\angle ABC$ is 55°, what is the measure of $\angle BTC$?

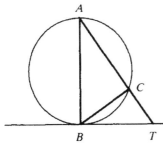

F. 35° J. 65°
G. 45° K. 90°
H. 55°

33. A city recently raised its sales tax from 5% of the purchase price to 6.5%. How much additional sales tax will result from this increase on a purchase with a pre-tax total price of $38.00?

A. $.57   D. $3.04
B. $1.90   E. $5.70
C. $2.47

34. The sum of two numbers is 12. If x represents one number, which expression below represents the product of the two numbers?

F. $x(12 - x)$
G. $x(x - 12)$
H. $x(12 + x)$
J. $(12 - x)(12 + x)$
K. $(x - 12)(x + 12)$

35. In the figure below, A, E, and B are collinear, and $\angle DEC$ is a right angle. If the measures of $\angle AED$ and $\angle CEB$ are in the ratio 3:2, what is the measure, in degrees, of $\angle AED$?

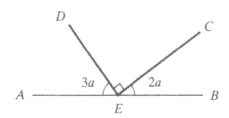

A. 18° D. 45°
B. 30° E. 54°
C. 36°

36. As the value of x increases from 0° to 90°, which of the following describes the behavior of $\sin x$ and $\cos x$?

F. Both $\sin x$ and $\cos x$ remain the same.
G. Both $\sin x$ and $\cos x$ increase.
H. Both $\sin x$ and $\cos x$ decrease.
J. Cos x decreases and sin x increases.
K. Cos x increases and sin x decreases.

37. Which of the following expressions characterizes exactly the real values for x that are solutions for the inequality

$3(x - 3) - 5x > 2x + 3?$

A. $x > 2$ D. $x > -\dfrac{3}{2}$

B. $x > \dfrac{3}{2}$ E. $x < -3$

C. $x > -3$

38. Which of the following is the graph determined by the equation $3x - 5y = 18$?

F.
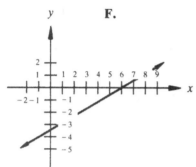

G.
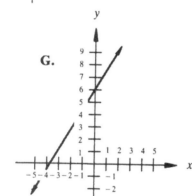

H.
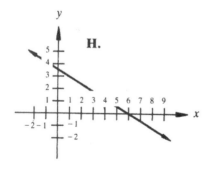

J.
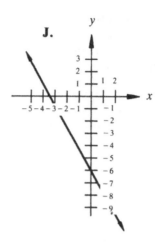

K.
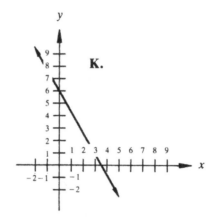

39. When the sum of $(2x - 1)$ and $(5 - 3x)$ is subtracted from $2(x + 1)$, the result is:

A. $3x + 6$
B. $3x - 2$
C. $3x - 3$
D. $6 - 3x$
E. $2 - 3x$

40. Which of the following expressions describes all real values for x that are solutions for the inequality $1 - x > -3$?

F. $x < 2$
G. $x < 3$
H. $x < 4$
J. $x > 3$
K. $x > 4$

41. In $\triangle ABC$ below, $\overline{CD}$ is perpendicular to $\overline{AB}$. If $\overline{AC}$ is 10 units long, $\overline{BC}$ is 5 units long, and $\overline{DB}$ is 3 units long, how many units long is $\overline{AD}$?

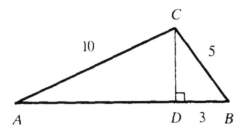

A. $\dfrac{16}{3}$

B. 6

C. 8

D. $2\sqrt{21}$

E. $4\sqrt{6}$

42. Which of the following is an equation of the line with slope 0 passing through the point with (x, y) coordinates $(1, 3)$?

F. $y = x + 2$

G. $y = 3$

H. $y = -3$

J. $x = 1$

K. $y = 3x$

43. The average (arithmetic mean) high temperature in Leesburg during the last seven days was 70°. On three of those days the high temperature was 55°, and on two of those days the high temperature was 70°. On the other two days the high temperatures differed by 5°. What were the high temperatures of those two days?

A. 90° and 95°

B. 85° and 90°

C. 80° and 85°

D. 75° and 80°

E. 70° and 75°

44. For all $x \neq 2$, $(x^4 - 16) \div (x - 2) = $?

F. $x + 2$

G. $(x + 2)^2$

H. $(x - 2)^3$

J. $x^3 + 2x^2 + 4x + 8$

K. $x^3 + 6x^2 + 12x + 8$

45. Which of the five figures is a graph of $x = y^2 - 6y + 9$?

A.
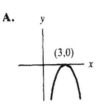

D.

B.
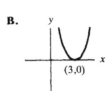

E.
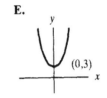

C.
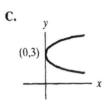

46. A painter purchased 38 gallons of paint to paint the apartments in a small building. If the job took only 73% of the paint, how many gallons were unused?

A. 9.74

B. 10.26

C. 10.74

D. 11.26

E. 30

165

ANSWER SHEET
For ACT Mathematics Practice Test A

Name _____

1. (A) (B) (C) (D) (E)
2. (F) (G) (H) (J) (K)
3. (A) (B) (C) (D) (E)
4. (F) (G) (H) (J) (K)
5. (A) (B) (C) (D) (E)
6. (F) (G) (H) (J) (K)
7. (A) (B) (C) (D) (E)
8. (F) (G) (H) (J) (K)
9. (A) (B) (C) (D) (E)
10. (F) (G) (H) (J) (K)
11. (A) (B) (C) (D) (E)
12. (F) (G) (H) (J) (K)
13. (A) (B) (C) (D) (E)
14. (F) (G) (H) (J) (K)
15. (A) (B) (C) (D) (E)
16. (F) (G) (H) (J) (K)
17. (A) (B) (C) (D) (E)
18. (F) (G) (H) (J) (K)
19. (A) (B) (C) (D) (E)
20. (F) (G) (H) (J) (K)
21. (A) (B) (C) (D) (E)
22. (F) (G) (H) (J) (K)
23. (A) (B) (C) (D) (E)
24. (F) (G) (H) (J) (K)
25. (A) (B) (C) (D) (E)

26. (F) (G) (H) (J) (K)
27. (A) (B) (C) (D) (E)
28. (F) (G) (H) (J) (K)
29. (A) (B) (C) (D) (E)
30 (F) (G) (H) (J) (K)
31. (A) (B) (C) (D) (E)
32. (F) (G) (H) (J) (K)
33. (A) (B) (C) (D) (E)
34. (F) (G) (H) (J) (K)
35. (A) (B) (C) (D) (E)
36. (F) (G) (H) (J) (K)
37. (A) (B) (C) (D) (E)
38. (F) (G) (H) (J) (K)
39. (A) (B) (C) (D) (E)
40. (F) (G) (H) (J) (K)
41. (A) (B) (C) (D) (E)
42. (F) (G) (H) (J) (K)
43. (A) (B) (C) (D) (E)
44. (F) (G) (H) (J) (K)
45. (A) (B) (C) (D) (E)
46. (F) (G) (H) (J) (K)
47. (A) (B) (C) (D) (E)
48. (F) (G) (H) (J) (K)
49. (A) (B) (C) (D) (E)
50. (F) (G) (H) (J) (K)

51. (A) (B) (C) (D) (E)
52. (F) (G) (H) (J) (K)
53. (A) (B) (C) (D) (E)
54. (F) (G) (H) (J) (K)
55. (A) (B) (C) (D) (E)
56. (F) (G) (H) (J) (K)
57. (A) (B) (C) (D) (E)
58. (F) (G) (H) (J) (K)
59. (A) (B) (C) (D) (E)
60. (F) (G) (H) (J) (K)

This page may be reproduced as needed.

ANSWER SHEET
For ACT Mathematics Practice Test B

Name _____

1. Ⓐ Ⓑ Ⓒ Ⓓ Ⓔ
2. Ⓕ Ⓖ Ⓗ Ⓙ Ⓚ
3. Ⓐ Ⓑ Ⓒ Ⓓ Ⓔ
4. Ⓕ Ⓖ Ⓗ Ⓙ Ⓚ
5. Ⓐ Ⓑ Ⓒ Ⓓ Ⓔ
6. Ⓕ Ⓖ Ⓗ Ⓙ Ⓚ
7. Ⓐ Ⓑ Ⓒ Ⓓ Ⓔ
8. Ⓕ Ⓖ Ⓗ Ⓙ Ⓚ
9. Ⓐ Ⓑ Ⓒ Ⓓ Ⓔ
10. Ⓕ Ⓖ Ⓗ Ⓙ Ⓚ
11. Ⓐ Ⓑ Ⓒ Ⓓ Ⓔ
12. Ⓕ Ⓖ Ⓗ Ⓙ Ⓚ
13. Ⓐ Ⓑ Ⓒ Ⓓ Ⓔ
14. Ⓕ Ⓖ Ⓗ Ⓙ Ⓚ
15. Ⓐ Ⓑ Ⓒ Ⓓ Ⓔ
16. Ⓕ Ⓖ Ⓗ Ⓙ Ⓚ
17. Ⓐ Ⓑ Ⓒ Ⓓ Ⓔ
18. Ⓕ Ⓖ Ⓗ Ⓙ Ⓚ
19. Ⓐ Ⓑ Ⓒ Ⓓ Ⓔ
20. Ⓕ Ⓖ Ⓗ Ⓙ Ⓚ
21. Ⓐ Ⓑ Ⓒ Ⓓ Ⓔ
22. Ⓕ Ⓖ Ⓗ Ⓙ Ⓚ
23. Ⓐ Ⓑ Ⓒ Ⓓ Ⓔ
24. Ⓕ Ⓖ Ⓗ Ⓙ Ⓚ
25. Ⓐ Ⓑ Ⓒ Ⓓ Ⓔ

26. Ⓕ Ⓖ Ⓗ Ⓙ Ⓚ
27. Ⓐ Ⓑ Ⓒ Ⓓ Ⓔ
28. Ⓕ Ⓖ Ⓗ Ⓙ Ⓚ
29. Ⓐ Ⓑ Ⓒ Ⓓ Ⓔ
30. Ⓕ Ⓖ Ⓗ Ⓙ Ⓚ
31. Ⓐ Ⓑ Ⓒ Ⓓ Ⓔ
32. Ⓕ Ⓖ Ⓗ Ⓙ Ⓚ
33. Ⓐ Ⓑ Ⓒ Ⓓ Ⓔ
34. Ⓕ Ⓖ Ⓗ Ⓙ Ⓚ
35. Ⓐ Ⓑ Ⓒ Ⓓ Ⓔ
36. Ⓕ Ⓖ Ⓗ Ⓙ Ⓚ
37. Ⓐ Ⓑ Ⓒ Ⓓ Ⓔ
38. Ⓕ Ⓖ Ⓗ Ⓙ Ⓚ
39. Ⓐ Ⓑ Ⓒ Ⓓ Ⓔ
40. Ⓕ Ⓖ Ⓗ Ⓙ Ⓚ
41. Ⓐ Ⓑ Ⓒ Ⓓ Ⓔ
42. Ⓕ Ⓖ Ⓗ Ⓙ Ⓚ
43. Ⓐ Ⓑ Ⓒ Ⓓ Ⓔ
44. Ⓕ Ⓖ Ⓗ Ⓙ Ⓚ
45. Ⓐ Ⓑ Ⓒ Ⓓ Ⓔ
46. Ⓕ Ⓖ Ⓗ Ⓙ Ⓚ
47. Ⓐ Ⓑ Ⓒ Ⓓ Ⓔ
48. Ⓕ Ⓖ Ⓗ Ⓙ Ⓚ
49. Ⓐ Ⓑ Ⓒ Ⓓ Ⓔ
50. Ⓕ Ⓖ Ⓗ Ⓙ Ⓚ

51. Ⓐ Ⓑ Ⓒ Ⓓ Ⓔ
52. Ⓕ Ⓖ Ⓗ Ⓙ Ⓚ
53. Ⓐ Ⓑ Ⓒ Ⓓ Ⓔ
54. Ⓕ Ⓖ Ⓗ Ⓙ Ⓚ
55. Ⓐ Ⓑ Ⓒ Ⓓ Ⓔ
56. Ⓕ Ⓖ Ⓗ Ⓙ Ⓚ
57. Ⓐ Ⓑ Ⓒ Ⓓ Ⓔ
58. Ⓕ Ⓖ Ⓗ Ⓙ Ⓚ
59. Ⓐ Ⓑ Ⓒ Ⓓ Ⓔ
60. Ⓕ Ⓖ Ⓗ Ⓙ Ⓚ

ANSWER SHEET
For ACT Mathematics Practice Test C

Name _____

1. Ⓐ Ⓑ Ⓒ Ⓓ Ⓔ	26. Ⓕ Ⓖ Ⓗ Ⓙ Ⓚ	51. Ⓐ Ⓑ Ⓒ Ⓓ Ⓔ
2. Ⓕ Ⓖ Ⓗ Ⓙ Ⓚ	27. Ⓐ Ⓑ Ⓒ Ⓓ Ⓔ	52. Ⓕ Ⓖ Ⓗ Ⓙ Ⓚ
3. Ⓐ Ⓑ Ⓒ Ⓓ Ⓔ	28. Ⓕ Ⓖ Ⓗ Ⓙ Ⓚ	53. Ⓐ Ⓑ Ⓒ Ⓓ Ⓔ
4. Ⓕ Ⓖ Ⓗ Ⓙ Ⓚ	29. Ⓐ Ⓑ Ⓒ Ⓓ Ⓔ	54. Ⓕ Ⓖ Ⓗ Ⓙ Ⓚ
5. Ⓐ Ⓑ Ⓒ Ⓓ Ⓔ	30 Ⓕ Ⓖ Ⓗ Ⓙ Ⓚ	55. Ⓐ Ⓑ Ⓒ Ⓓ Ⓔ
6. Ⓕ Ⓖ Ⓗ Ⓙ Ⓚ	31. Ⓐ Ⓑ Ⓒ Ⓓ Ⓔ	56. Ⓕ Ⓖ Ⓗ Ⓙ Ⓚ
7. Ⓐ Ⓑ Ⓒ Ⓓ Ⓔ	32. Ⓕ Ⓖ Ⓗ Ⓙ Ⓚ	57. Ⓐ Ⓑ Ⓒ Ⓓ Ⓔ
8. Ⓕ Ⓖ Ⓗ Ⓙ Ⓚ	33. Ⓐ Ⓑ Ⓒ Ⓓ Ⓔ	58. Ⓕ Ⓖ Ⓗ Ⓙ Ⓚ
9. Ⓐ Ⓑ Ⓒ Ⓓ Ⓔ	34. Ⓕ Ⓖ Ⓗ Ⓙ Ⓚ	59. Ⓐ Ⓑ Ⓒ Ⓓ Ⓔ
10. Ⓕ Ⓖ Ⓗ Ⓙ Ⓚ	35. Ⓐ Ⓑ Ⓒ Ⓓ Ⓔ	60. Ⓕ Ⓖ Ⓗ Ⓙ Ⓚ
11. Ⓐ Ⓑ Ⓒ Ⓓ Ⓔ	36. Ⓕ Ⓖ Ⓗ Ⓙ Ⓚ	
12. Ⓕ Ⓖ Ⓗ Ⓙ Ⓚ	37. Ⓐ Ⓑ Ⓒ Ⓓ Ⓔ	
13. Ⓐ Ⓑ Ⓒ Ⓓ Ⓔ	38. Ⓕ Ⓖ Ⓗ Ⓙ Ⓚ	
14. Ⓕ Ⓖ Ⓗ Ⓙ Ⓚ	39. Ⓐ Ⓑ Ⓒ Ⓓ Ⓔ	
15. Ⓐ Ⓑ Ⓒ Ⓓ Ⓔ	40. Ⓕ Ⓖ Ⓗ Ⓙ Ⓚ	
16. Ⓕ Ⓖ Ⓗ Ⓙ Ⓚ	41. Ⓐ Ⓑ Ⓒ Ⓓ Ⓔ	
17. Ⓐ Ⓑ Ⓒ Ⓓ Ⓔ	42. Ⓕ Ⓖ Ⓗ Ⓙ Ⓚ	
18. Ⓕ Ⓖ Ⓗ Ⓙ Ⓚ	43. Ⓐ Ⓑ Ⓒ Ⓓ Ⓔ	
19. Ⓐ Ⓑ Ⓒ Ⓓ Ⓔ	44. Ⓕ Ⓖ Ⓗ Ⓙ Ⓚ	
20. Ⓕ Ⓖ Ⓗ Ⓙ Ⓚ	45. Ⓐ Ⓑ Ⓒ Ⓓ Ⓔ	
21. Ⓐ Ⓑ Ⓒ Ⓓ Ⓔ	46. Ⓕ Ⓖ Ⓗ Ⓙ Ⓚ	
22. Ⓕ Ⓖ Ⓗ Ⓙ Ⓚ	47. Ⓐ Ⓑ Ⓒ Ⓓ Ⓔ	
23. Ⓐ Ⓑ Ⓒ Ⓓ Ⓔ	48. Ⓕ Ⓖ Ⓗ Ⓙ Ⓚ	
24. Ⓕ Ⓖ Ⓗ Ⓙ Ⓚ	49. Ⓐ Ⓑ Ⓒ Ⓓ Ⓔ	
25. Ⓐ Ⓑ Ⓒ Ⓓ Ⓔ	50. Ⓕ Ⓖ Ⓗ Ⓙ Ⓚ	

This page may be reproduced as needed.